PRIVACY:
ASSESSING THE RISK

By Kim Hargraves, CPA, CISA
Susan B. Lione, CIA, CCSA, CGAP
Kerry L. Shackelford, CPA, CISA, CCP
Peter C. Tilton, CPA, CISA

This report is part of the *Systems Assurance and Control* project

The Institute of Internal Auditors Research Foundation

ISBN 0-89413-502-3
03024 04/03
First Printing

CONTENTS

ABOUT THE AUTHORS

Kim Hargraves, CPA, CISA, is the IT Audit Senior Manager at Microsoft Corporation. She manages the business/IT integration team for Microsoft Corporation. This team is engaged in audit support initiatives to assess systems risk and perform audits across all of Microsoft's business units, and provide integrated systems audit support services for operations audits, systems development, and process reengineering. In addition, she is responsible for internal audit's privacy assurance initiative and works closely with Microsoft's Corporate Privacy Group in strategic areas in order to enhance the program and the company's ability to ensure compliance with related laws, regulations, corporate directives, and best practices. Ms. Hargraves specializes in security and privacy, application development audits, and SAP audit and controls. Her past experiences include SAP security consulting and financial auditing for PricewaterhouseCoopers, and financial analysis for Specialty Brands.

Susan Lione, CIA, CCSA, CGAP, is Assistant Vice President of Research at The Institute of Internal Auditors (IIA) in Altamonte Springs, Florida. She has worked at The IIA since 1993. Prior to joining The IIA, Ms. Lione was Senior Auditor at Martin Marietta (now known as Lockheed Martin), as well as auditor for the Naval Audit Service in Jacksonville, Washington, DC, and Orlando. She has over 10 years of internal auditing experience and specializes in operational, compliance, and financial audits. Ms. Lione recently retired from the Air Force, having completed over 20 years of active duty and reserve service. Ms. Lione received her B.S. degree in accounting from Old Dominion University, and her M.B.A. from Florida Institute of Technology.

Kerry Shackleford, CPA, CISA, CCP, is the General Manager and sole employee of KLS Consulting LLC, a Colorado limited liability company formed in 2002. He has 17+ years of experience consulting with clients on matters of business and technology risk assessment and management. Prior to starting this new venture, Mr. Shackleford led Arthur Andersen's worldwide privacy and data protection practice. Mr. Shackleford has a working knowledge of fair information practices generally and the requirements of specific U.S. privacy regulations such as GLBA, HIPAA, and the US/EU Safe Harbor program. Mr. Shackleford holds a bachelor of arts degree in computer science and a concentration in accounting from Baylor University in Waco, Texas.

Peter Tilton, CPA, CISA, is the Director of IT Audit Services at Microsoft Corporation. He leads several Internal Audit Services initiatives to assess IT risk and strategy across the company, including worldwide security policies and practices, IT application and infrastructure security, electronic commerce, and integrated systems audit support services for operations audits, systems development, and process reengineering. Mr. Tilton's group also performs a key role within Microsoft Internal Audit Services to help envision and develop technology solutions to manage the audit process more effectively. He is a member of The IIA's Advanced Technology Committee, and recently led the development of *Systems Assurance and Control* (*SAC*), The IIA's framework and guidance to help understand, assess, monitor, and mitigate technology risks. Before joining Microsoft in 1996, Mr. Tilton worked for Price Waterhouse in Denver.

ACKNOWLEDGMENTS

The IIA Research Foundation (IIA RF) acknowledges and greatly appreciates the sponsorship, participation, assistance, and general cooperation of the people and organizations involved in the *Systems Assurance and Control (SAC)* project. The IIA relies on its members worldwide to support progress of the profession of internal auditing — our motto is "Progress Through Sharing" — and this project exemplifies that motto.

We express appreciation to Kim Hargraves, Kerry Shackelford, and Peter Tilton who volunteered their time and expertise to author this report on Privacy, and to Microsoft Corporation for providing staff and resources to complete this work.

Many other individuals also contributed their time and expert insights to this project. Our thanks to the Privacy review team, the SAC project review team, and to The IIA Research Foundation Trustees and Board of Research Advisors who provided their support and assistance.

CHAPTER 1
INTRODUCTION AND
EXECUTIVE SUMMARY

Introduction

The objective of this report is to provide relevant information on privacy and data protection worldwide, discuss approaches to evaluating and managing privacy risk, and the auditor's role in privacy. This report does not address all of the specific privacy regulations, though it is shaped around a global perspective. Its primary focus is on Internet/Web-related technologies and applications and, to a certain extent, back-office information systems. There are many other privacy-related issues with "offline" data collected and used through other means, such as fax, mail-in registrations and warranties, customer phone support, etc., that are not discussed herein.

This report is based on a set of common principles and legal, regulatory, self-regulatory, and effective practices used to define risk management and mitigation strategies to manage privacy risk on a global basis. It outlines the evolution of privacy legislation and major developments relevant to the privacy framework, with a primary focus on the US/EU Safe Harbor agreement as a common set of principles that generally define a universal approach to privacy laws, regulations, and considerations. Chapter 2, Privacy Legislation, contains examples of privacy and data protection measures around the world.

This is an evolving area and difficult to keep up with. For example, in late 2001 when it appeared the U.S. was moving toward omnibus privacy legislation, the Bush administration's new chairman of the U.S. Federal Trade Commission (FTC) announced that it was "too soon" to recommend broad-based online privacy legislation. Instead, the chairman stated he favored the enforcement of current laws and self-regulation. His privacy agenda called for a 50 percent increase in FTC resources dedicated to privacy protection. He focused the FTC on improved privacy complaint handling, more protection for consumers from unsolicited commercial e-mail (spam), telemarketing, pretexting, and identity theft, with increased enforcement of privacy policies and existing laws such as the Fair Credit Reporting Act (FCRA) and the Children's Online Privacy Protection Act (COPPA). Where the U.S. federal regulations stop, states are stepping in. For instance, California recently passed SB 1386 requiring organizations to disclose security breaches where personal information was acquired by an unauthorized person.

There are a variety of laws and regulations developing worldwide. Diligent efforts are required to stay current with the rapidly changing legal environments in many countries. However, there are generally accepted principles, appropriate for framing the privacy issue. An organization trying to manage privacy globally may have a difficult time operating in compliance with the letter of the law in every country where they have a presence. Initially, adopting a general standard designed to meet the majority of regulations worldwide or in specific countries where they do business may be the best option. Specific considerations should be made for countries with more restrictive regulations.

The information herein is designed to provide enterprises with a global perspective on the most important privacy risks and issues, and the general tools and techniques that might be employed to effectively assess and manage privacy risk. There are many sources of information that should be consulted for historic context, country specific laws, standards, and practices.

Why Should Businesses Care About Privacy?

Privacy has many impacts and far-reaching effects that the enterprise should consider in the scope of risk management programs. High emphasis is being placed on privacy laws and regulations that affect organizations doing business in certain countries. There are also numerous customer trust and related issues that could have an impact on the business viability of many organizations. The major considerations include:

- **Legal and Regulatory Factors** — Where regulations exist, organizations not compliant with privacy laws are exposed to substantial fines and other legal remedies. The current intensity of the public and government focus on privacy issues and related industry self-regulatory and advocacy trends indicate increasing legislation and scrutiny of privacy practices.

- **Data Flows and Transfers** — One of the most obvious considerations outside European Union (EU) countries is that, under EU law, European organizations cannot export data to countries that do not meet its minimum privacy protection standards. The negative impact on a noncompliant country or organization within a country could be devastating.

- **Impact on Revenues and Brands** — Ultimately, privacy law violations and publicized incidents could have a negative impact on an organization's image and trustworthiness, impairing revenues and future ability to build revenue opportunities for products and services.

- **Public Relations and Media Exploits** — Consumer trust and confidence are influenced by media reports, legal actions and complaints by privacy advocacy groups. In some cases, such groups exploit privacy violations and incidents, creating greater public concern.

- **Stock Price** — Real or perceived privacy violations, with respect to an organization's posted/public policies and legal/regulatory considerations, have in the past had a significant negative impact on the stock price.

Privacy — Global Perspective

The constitutional frameworks of many countries recognize privacy as a fundamental human right; in some, the issue is still hotly debated. In most international treaties and agreements on human rights, privacy is fundamental to human dignity and other values such as freedom of association and freedom of speech.

The global privacy landscape involves legislative, regulatory, and cultural considerations, which often have overlapping or similar requirements that range from generally accepted to restrictive in certain countries. Recently, growing concerns over globalization of business due to the Internet and other trends has meant that newer laws and regulations commonly include specific rights to access and control one's personal information. Privacy provisions range from the sanctity of the home and confidentiality of communications to those specific access rights.

Most industrialized countries have privacy and data protection acts. Nearly 50 countries and jurisdictions have enacted, or are in the process of enacting, privacy and data protection laws. Generally these laws address past governmental abuses, promote electronic commerce, or ensure compatibility with international standards from organizations such as the European Union, the Council of Europe, and the Organization for Economic Cooperation and Development (OECD).

Defining Privacy

Privacy definitions vary widely depending on country, culture, political environment, and legal framework. In many countries, privacy is synonymous with data protection. Outside this context, privacy implies the extent to which society and governments can intrude into an individual's private affairs. The U.S. Constitution did not provide citizens a basic human right to privacy, though it did protect citizens from the government itself through the Fourth Amendment:

> *"The right of the people to be secure in their persons, houses, papers, and effects, against unreasonable searches and seizures, shall not be violated, and no Warrants shall issue, but upon probable cause, supported by Oath or affirmation, and particularly describing the place to be searched, and the persons or things to be seized."*
>
> — Amendment IV, The Bill of Rights (1791 - 2001)

Instead, the U.S. has taken a more sectoral or industry-specific approach, allowing a wide range of activity unless specifically prohibited. The U.S. also relies upon self-regulation.

The preamble to the Australian Privacy Charter, as noted by the Electronic Privacy Information Center and Privacy International (EPIC/PI), provides a relevant context for purposes of this privacy discussion:

> *A free and democratic society requires respect for the autonomy of individuals, and limits on the power of both state and private organizations to intrude on that autonomy... Privacy is a key value which underpins human dignity and other key values such as freedom of association and freedom of speech... Privacy is a basic human right, and the reasonable expectation of every person.*

Personally Identifiable Information (PII)

Privacy generally refers to information that can be associated with a specific individual, or that has identifying characteristics that might be combined with other information to do so. PII is the definitive term that should be used consistently when referring to an individual's personally identifiable information in the privacy context.

Information considered *sensitive* is included in PII. This term is generally accepted or defined in legal terms to require a higher standard of protection. Sensitive data includes individual preferences, habits, confidential financial or health information, or other personal information. It is important to note that the context of the privacy issue and related laws and regulations is the *individual*, not to be confused with the *consumer, customer,* or other terms that identify a person's role or function. An individual might be a consumer, corporate employee, sales account contact, and so forth.

Information that identifies an individual and related data defines the privacy context. Information captured about a sales contact in a sales management system, for instance, would most likely be subject to all privacy considerations.

Legal Frameworks

Legal frameworks worldwide have generally not anticipated the pervasive role of technology in people's daily lives, nor how information would be collected and used by private sector organizations, nor how the Internet facilitates governments' collection and use of information about individuals' activities and communications. While the Internet has changed the quantity and quality of information, business and government practices, standards, laws, and regulations have not kept pace ensuring individuals' privacy.

Impact of the Internet Information Age

While the right to privacy was born well before the information age, the impact of technology has brought the issue to the forefront. Technological developments that have led to today's privacy issues include the following:

- **Computer Processing** — Computers make it possible to retrieve, process, and share information with more people much faster. Earlier manual record keeping provided some privacy simply because it was difficult to disseminate personal and private information.

- **Databases and Data Warehouses** — Database management systems capable of storing, searching, and retrieving vast amounts of data rapidly; and, cheap, plentiful storage enabled the building of large data warehouses containing personal and private information.

- **Network Communications** — Information stored in databases posed less of a threat to privacy until it became so easily shared. As network technology evolved from local area to wide area coverage to the Internet, ease of collection and dissemination of information increased dramatically.

- **Electronic Document Imaging and Storage Media** — Records to authorize, initiate, and process transactions are routinely scanned by copying mechanisms which convert the "image" into bits of data that can be recreated virtually anywhere, used to support individual decisions, internal corporate processes (e.g., claims processes, adjudications, etc.), and litigation.

The Internet has increased the amount of information about its users that is in circulation. When a user browses a Web site, for example, his or her computer (the "client") provides various types of information to the Web site operator's computer (the "host"). This includes the client's Internet Protocol ("IP") address and basic technical information (called "chatter") about its browser, operating system and hardware platform, plus the browsing activity, including time and date of visit and the requested Uniform Resource Locator ("URL").

Web sites that use "cookies" and browsers that allow them can leave a trail of activities in the form of data files left on an individual's computer. As users browse particular Web sites, the host computer may send a data file, or "cookie," to the client to store certain information, such as user IDs or language preferences, that can be recognized and supplemented on repeat visits. Through use of these technologies, the host can collect information on the Web pages the client views, creating a "click stream" trail of how the client uses the host's site.

Collecting this information enables Web site operators to provide enhanced user experiences. Its ready availability allows online organizations to tailor content to individual preferences, provide personalized services, and improve Web site offerings. With access to information about Web site users, online firms can improve inventory management and direct marketing activities, increasing productivity and cutting costs. This, in turn, results in even better service and lower prices for Internet users.

But it also raises privacy concerns. Isolated pieces of information collected may have little meaning, but when aggregated, reveal patterns of behavior. As consumers take advantage of the convenience offered by the Internet, their online profiles become much more substantive. Wireless applications can track physical location; enhanced television and cable service delivery can monitor programming choices; and consumer appliance protocols can gather information on favorite foods, daily schedules, and other facets of daily life. Such developments make Internet users apprehensive about protection of their privacy when online.

Brick-and-mortar retailers have for years used direct-mail advertising and telemarketing, but some would argue that unwanted mail can be thrown away, and phone calls ended with little or no cost to the individual. Not true of unsolicited e-mail and faxes; they require download time and disk space, or in the case of faxes, fax paper. The relative newness of Internet use by consumers, coupled with a lack of comfort in cyberspace, has created an atmosphere of distrust.

The Internet's potential as a medium for social and economic advancement depends largely on building and ensuring trust online. People will not take full advantage of it if they believe the information they provide will be insecure or used or disclosed in ways of which they do not approve nor expect. These paired issues — security and privacy — pose unique challenges to building trust on the Internet, and both must be addressed to foster the growth of electronic commerce.

The self-interest of the various constituencies that comprise the Internet — users, consumer advocates and rights groups, industry, and government — means movement toward adoption of technologies, self-regulation, and/or laws and regulations to provide individuals with greater control over personal information and privacy. Leading providers of e-commerce software and services are committed to creating a trusted environment for Internet users; protecting online privacy is at the core of this commitment.

Private sector efforts may only be successful if governments worldwide support them effectively. Cooperative efforts on an international level may be essential to resolve online privacy concerns and create an Internet environment that truly promotes consumer trust.

Public and Private Sector Cooperation

A comprehensive response to online privacy concerns in the ever-changing Internet environment requires close cooperation between private and public sectors. This effort should promote market-driven technological solutions, recognize privacy principles around which broad consensus exists, and develop legal frameworks to support such solutions and principles. The critical roles each sector can play are discussed below.

Role of the Private Sector

Private sector efforts may be well suited to solving privacy-related problems on the Internet, because generally their initiatives can respond more quickly than legislative solutions. Private sector mechanisms are consumer-driven, thus more likely to give users a choice of solutions based on individual preferences. Requirements that are more or less intense than users want are unavoidable in government regulations, which typically are one dimensional in nature. On the other hand, there are many who will violate privacy for various reasons or advantages in the absence of specific and restrictive privacy regulations and related sanctions.

The private sector has taken significant steps to address online privacy concerns. The high-tech industry has developed a range of inexpensive, easy-to-use products giving consumers extensive control over personal data. Increased efforts to educate them on the diverse solutions available and how they protect privacy online are needed; such education may be the most effective way to protect privacy. Many organizations have adopted privacy practices to promote trust; some have initiatives to promote online privacy that require adherence to data protection principles.

The private sector must take greater responsibility for market-based solutions to online privacy problems. Solutions must reflect a range of preferences made available so consumers worldwide can readily tailor online experiences. It must also adopt voluntary, flexible, yet effective, online privacy practices more widely. Industry groups have been proactive in encouraging operators to follow privacy principles; however, more work must be done.

Role of the Public Sector

Governments need to work together across borders to address privacy concerns that have no borders. Disparate national online privacy regimes may affect international online trade adversely by imposing inconsistent legal obligations on businesses. Stakeholders in the Internet environment should consider supporting efforts to forge international consensus on a balanced approach, promoting market-driven technological solutions and public sector legal frameworks that support such solutions.

Online privacy concerns can only be resolved effectively with the active participation of governments around the world. Working with the private sector, they must identify online privacy concerns; develop basic principles to guide potential resolution; and encourage private sector solutions that further those principles. By facilitating private sector initiatives and supporting solutions based on them, governments can help resolve concerns in ways that are responsive, flexible, and adaptive to the nature of the Internet itself.

At times, governments will augment private sector privacy efforts through legislation and policy. Hopefully, this will provide a workable framework for online privacy concern identification and resolution. The Safe Harbor privacy principles agreed to by the EU and the U.S. perform this function. Legal safe harbors are useful since they encourage the private sector to abide by a set of privacy principles and pursue broader public policy goals. This benefits users while giving the private sector a strong incentive to devise self-regulatory mechanisms that work.

When governments consider regulation, it may be important to develop a framework that protects privacy without discouraging Internet growth. Far-reaching regulation could go farther than targeting discrete privacy concerns, and has the potential of stifling Internet growth and optimization.

Consumer Perspectives

Surveys about privacy concerns are conducted regularly. A recent poll confirms that Americans care about privacy. More than half the respondents favor some public policy on how personal information can be collected and used on the Internet. One in three are not comfortable with their online actions being profiled, and four in five are not comfortable with online activities being merged with PII, such as income, driver's license, credit data, and medical status. Other polls in the U.S. identify consistent concerns; it is reasonable to assume Internet users worldwide would react similarly:

- Almost two-thirds of non-Internet users would be more likely to start using it if the privacy of their personal information and communications were protected.
- Privacy is the number one reason individuals choose to stay off the Internet, well ahead of concerns with costs, complicated technology, and unsolicited commercial e-mail.
- While varying by survey, generally more than half of respondents believe government should regulate collection of personal information over the Internet.
- More than three-quarters of survey respondents are concerned with using a credit card to make an online purchase.
- To protect their privacy, significant numbers of Internet users falsify information online.

- Tracking people's use of the Internet and the sale of personal information were cited consistently as some of the most pressing privacy issues.
- Junk mail is often in the top three in terms of overall privacy concerns and it generated the largest number of anecdotal complaints.

In response, a minority of informed or educated users are:

- Only doing business with reputable organizations they know and trust.
- Opting out of receiving marketing solicitations.
- Using secure Web sites.
- Disabling cookies (although these users realize cookies are necessary for some Web site functionality).
- Preventing Internet access to personal files.
- Protecting their passwords.
- Encrypting their files.

The Internet will continue to empower consumers as they have more controls over how they pay for what they buy, and to let sellers compete for their business. Organizations may meet specific preferences of individuals while still tailoring marketing based on personal information about shopping habits, likes and dislikes, as well as demographics and other characteristics. This exchange of information will continue to raise potential privacy and security concerns.

Consumer Expectations: Anonymity

When individuals surf the Internet, they expect anonymity. But the Internet technologies used often leave a trail of details of an individual's online activities. The data may be captured by Web sites, employers, or the Internet service provider (ISP) used for access. Transactional data can provide a "profile" of an individual's preferences, habits, and shopping patterns. Technologies such as cookies can be misused to track an individual's specific activities to allow customizing content and advertising.

Governments are interested in this data as a major consumer of personal information about their constituents. Many wireless devices and networks collect information about the location of a person operating the device, even when the device is not in operation. The government may use such data for surveillance while the private sector considers how to use this information for profit, such as offering location-based services through a user's cellular phone.

Consumer Expectations: Confidentiality

When people send e-mail, they expect only its intended recipient will read it. However, unencrypted e-mail is reasonably simple to capture and read as it traverses the Internet. When using e-mail on an office computer, it is both possible and legal for the organization to monitor and archive all e-mail, as well as any other PII stored on organization resources.

An e-mail message may be handled by many different entities, and may cross international borders even if it is a domestic communication. The rogue action or policy of a single computer network can compromise the confidentiality or integrity of information. Similarly, hackers, terrorists, criminals, and others can systematically capture and distribute or simply corrupt this information.

As information is increasingly digitized, it is located on different networks, systems, and remote servers, including services that handle information on behalf of the user, such as MSN or AOL. Health-care information is used by providers and insurance companies to gain efficiencies in billing, prescription refills, insurance authorizations and payments, and other services. Privacy risks increase dramatically when sensitive information resides in multiple locations, business, networks, systems, and so forth.

Consumer Expectations: Fairness and Control

When the power of Internet technology to collect, aggregate, analyze, and distribute personal information is combined with potentially questionable business practices, individual privacy can be compromised. Although public scrutiny of such practices has raised the overall privacy standards of many organizations, individual information is still frequently used beyond the context of its original intended use.

When individuals provide information to a service provider, such as a merchant or doctor, they expect it to be used only in the context of the service provided. However, information generated is often used for a variety of other purposes without the user's consent. Incidents have occurred where personal health information was sold and used to target market drugs and alternative treatments to patients based on their condition. Regulations such as the Health Insurance Portability and Accountability Act (HIPAA) in the U.S. should curb such uses.

There are many other privacy-related issues with "offline" data collected and used through other means, such as fax, mail-in registrations, product warranties, customer phone support, and the like. Customer expectations conceptually are no different in online and offline data.

Increasing Consumer Confidence

Privacy is essentially a question of trust between the individual and the service provider. Trust is a powerful differentiator that can be leveraged as a competitive advantage as individuals become more knowledgeable of information practices. Managing privacy better than competitors through addressing customer fears around online commerce may remove the privacy concern as a deterrent to transacting business online.

Demonstrating a commitment to fair information practices and reliable, good practices in managing and protecting personal data can provide assurance to potential and existing customers. Assuring customers, related stakeholders, allies, and the public at large that a privacy policy and effective practices that achieve the objectives of the policy have been put into practice is a means of demonstrating that commitment. Being able to demonstrate this as a "routine business practice" can result in advantages in the long term. Alternatively, avoiding complaints of deceptive and unfair business practices can be seen as another benefit.

Privacy, Data Protection, and Information Security

Enterprise-wide information security will enable privacy through data protection, a secured infrastructure, detection and mitigation of intrusions, reduction of malicious attacks, and business continuity and disaster recovery.

Data protection and information security are synonymous within the privacy framework and related systems. Data protection defines principles, mandatory or voluntary, of effective practices to use, process, store, or disseminate personal information. The interpretation of *data protection* that is embodied in various laws and declarations worldwide generally requires that data is:

- Fairly and lawfully processed.
- Processed for limited purposes.
- Adequate, relevant, and not excessive.
- Accurate.
- Not kept longer than necessary.
- Processed in accordance with the data subject's rights.
- Secure.
- Not transferred to countries without adequate (comparable) protection.

Information security provides the technical mechanisms to enforce data protection rules in support of privacy policies, objectives, and requirements in applications, data stores, systems, and networks.

While it is possible, though unlikely, to have good security with poor privacy management, it is difficult to achieve real privacy without reasonable security. Information security is vital to the functioning of adequate privacy controls. By default, a secure system that restricts data from unauthorized individuals, and limits data to authorized individuals on an as-needed basis or as consistent with their job function, naturally provides adequate protections over PII.

CHAPTER 2
PRIVACY LEGISLATION

Introduction

The objective of this chapter is to provide an introduction to privacy and data protection regulations and legislation worldwide. It provides a brief history of privacy and data protection around the world to point out the origins of fair information practices. It also describes the evolution of privacy legislation and major developments relevant to the privacy framework, with a primary focus on the US/EU Safe Harbor agreement as a common set of principles that generally define a universal approach to privacy laws, regulations and considerations, or the evolution of privacy tenets through time.

While the chapter is shaped around a global perspective, it does not attempt to address all of the specific privacy regulations, because there are so many. It contains examples of privacy and data protection measures and activities around the world.

The leading legal, regulatory, self-regulatory, and effective practices are used in this report to define risk management and mitigation strategies to manage privacy risk on a global basis. A variety of laws and regulations are developing worldwide, and diligent efforts are required to stay current in the rapidly changing legal environments in many countries.

An organization trying to manage privacy globally may have a difficult time complying with the letter of the law in every country where they may have a presence. Initially, adopting a general standard designed to meet the majority of privacy regulations worldwide or in specific countries in which they do business may be the best option. Specific considerations should be made for countries with more restrictive regulations.

The information herein is designed to provide auditors and management with a global perspective of the most important legislative risks and issues. Other sources of information should be consulted for historic context, country specific laws, standards, and practices.

Approaches to Privacy Protection

Privacy International, an international advocacy and support group for privacy, has defined four major "models" for privacy protection. These models, discussed in the following paragraphs, can be complimentary or contradictory; in most countries several are used together, and in the countries that protect privacy most diligently, all of the models work together.

Comprehensive Laws

In many countries, there are general laws that govern the use, storage, transfer, and dissemination of personal information with an oversight body that ensures compliance. For most countries currently adopting data protection laws and regulations, this is the model used. The European Union provides an example in the case of the European Data Protection Directive.

Sectoral Laws

Some countries have opted to generally allow use of personal information unless specifically restricted by sectoral (industry) laws that govern data protection in certain industries, such as the financial or health-care sectors. In many countries, sectoral laws are used to complement general data protection provisions to provide more detailed protections for specific types of data. The U.S. legal framework is sectoral.

Self-regulation

In some countries, most notably the U.S., data protection is dependent on various forms of self-regulation. Advocacy groups, media watchdogs, and the private sector have developed a variety of self-regulatory initiatives partially to assuage consumer concerns and partially to forestall potentially onerous legislation or regulations that could impede the growth of electronic commerce.

Many businesses want to avoid legislation requiring privacy, hoping to succeed with self-regulatory models to allow advertising and direct marketing activities to consumers, while adhering to a reasonable code of conduct. Typically, they oppose the highest, most consumer-oriented levels of privacy protection. In addition, there are a number of industry groups and initiatives that advocate business self-regulatory efforts and provide services and methodologies to validate the effectiveness of an entity's privacy program independently (such as TRUSTe and the Better Business Bureau's BBBOnLine programs).

Privacy Technologies

Individuals have gained more control over privacy and security of personal information with the advent of privacy technologies and standards. These include programs and systems, referred to as privacy enabling technologies or privacy enhancing technologies, that provide varying degrees of privacy and security over communications and identity, including encryption, anonymous access, privacy preference disclosure programs, filtering solutions, and smart cards.

Global Governmental Privacy Activity

Privacy and data protection are worldwide issues. Organizations must recognize that the user community of Web sites is a worldwide group with unique cultural and legislative differences. The rights of individual citizens vary substantially from one country to another. Thinking about fair information practices has come from several international sources, discussed in the sections that follow.

Shortly after World War II, privacy was addressed in the 1948 United Nations Universal Declaration of Human Rights. Article 12 of the Declaration stated that, "No one shall be subjected to arbitrary interference with his privacy, family, home or correspondence, nor to attacks upon his honour and reputation. Everyone has the right to the protection of the law against such interference or attacks."

Interest in privacy rights and data protection increased throughout the 1960s and 1970s with the advent of increasing use of information technology. Given the data gathering and surveillance potential of computer systems, demands arose to develop rules governing collection and handling of personal information. Many countries developed new constitutions to reflect this right. Current legislation can be traced to early data protection laws, starting in Germany in 1970, and followed by Sweden (1973), the U.S. (1974), Germany again (1977), and France (1978).

Two important agreements evolved from these laws. The 1981 Council of Europe (COE) *Convention for the Protection of Individuals with regard to the Automatic Processing of Personal Data* and the Organization for Economic Cooperation and Development (OECD) *Guidelines on the Protection of Privacy and Transborder Flows of Personal Data* specify guidelines over handling electronic data. The guidelines are the basis for data protection laws in dozens of countries. They provide for data protection from collection to storage and dissemination, and include provisions for individuals to access and amend their data as a primary tenet.

Over 20 countries have adopted the COE convention and others have signed it, but have not yet committed it to law. The OECD guidelines have also been widely used in national legislation, even outside OECD countries. Based on the principles in these guidelines, the European Union (EU) developed the Directive on Data Protection ("the Directive") which became effective on October 25, 1998.

The Directive standardizes protection of data privacy for the European Union (Austria, Belgium, Denmark, Finland, France, Germany, Greece, Ireland, Italy, Luxembourg, Netherlands, Portugal, Spain, Sweden, and United Kingdom) citizens, while allowing for the free flow of information among member sites. Significant for the U.S. and other countries outside the EU, the Directive prohibits transfer of personally identifiable data to third countries that do not provide an "adequate" level of privacy protection (which roughly translates to comparable).

Currently, the Directive is the most far-reaching, established privacy guideline, and is influencing current and emerging privacy legislation. It contains fundamental, if not universal, principles for managing personal information and data protection, and is the basis for US/EU Safe Harbor, discussed below.

Countries at the forefront of privacy legislation and regulation outside the EU include Australia, Canada, Hong Kong, Japan, and New Zealand. They embrace technological progress and electronic commerce while still protecting and enhancing long-cherished fundamental rights through regulation. As eastern European countries join the EU, they are required to comply with the Directive. While specific and sometimes significant differences on certain points exist, the fundamental principles discussed previously are comparable to the Directive and the US/EU Safe Harbor Agreement.

The Organization for Economic Cooperation and Development (OECD)
http://www.oecd.org

The OECD is a Paris-based intergovernmental organization of 29 member countries, among the first to address the protection of personal data. The OECD is a forum in which governments can compare their experiences, discuss problems they share, and seek solutions that can be applied within their own national contexts. The OECD Web site offers numerous publications on e-commerce in a global marketplace.

In September 1980, the OECD published *Guidelines on the Protection of Privacy and Transborder Flows of Personal Data*. It represented a consensus on basic principles that could be built into existing national legislation, or serve as a basis for legislation in those countries which did not yet have it. The purpose was to harmonize national privacy legislation among member countries and, while upholding human rights, prevent interruptions in international flows of data. The principles of national application in Part Two contain the bedrock principles of privacy and data protection. Introduced briefly here, more information is available at the OECD Web site:

- **Collection Limitation Principle** — There should be limits to the collection of personal data, and any such data should be obtained by lawful and fair means and, where appropriate, with the knowledge or consent of the data subject.

- **Data Quality Principle** — Personal data should be relevant to the purposes for which they are to be used, and, to the extent necessary for those purposes, should be accurate, complete, and kept up-to-date.

- **Purpose Specification Principle** — The purposes for which personal data is collected should be specified not later than at the time of data collection and the subsequent use limited to the fulfillment of those purposes or such others as are not incompatible with those purposes and as are specified on each occasion of change of purpose.

- **Use Limitation Principle** — Personal data should not be disclosed, made available, or otherwise used for purposes other than those specified in accordance with the Purpose Specification Principle except: a) with the consent of the data subject; or b) by the authority of law.

- **Security Safeguards Principle** — Personal data should be protected by reasonable security safeguards against such risks as loss or unauthorized access, destruction, use, modification, or disclosure of data.

- **Openness Principle** — There should be a general policy of openness about developments, practices, and policies with respect to personal data. Means should be readily available to establish the existence and nature of personal data, and the main purposes of use, as well as the identity and usual residence of the data controller.

- **Individual Participation Principle** — An individual should have the right:
  (a) To obtain from a data controller, or other, confirmation of whether or not the data controller has data relating to him;
  (b) To have communicated to him data relating to him:
      - Within a reasonable time;
      - At a charge, if any, that is not excessive;
      - In a reasonable manner; and
      - In a form that is readily intelligible to him;
  (c) To be given reasons if a request made under subparagraphs *(a)* and *(b)* is denied, and to be able to challenge such denial; and
  (d) To challenge data relating to him and, if the challenge is successful to have the data erased, rectified, completed, or amended.

- **Accountability Principle** — A data controller should be accountable for complying with measures that give effect to the principles stated above.

Council of Europe (COE)
http://conventions.coe.int/treaty/EN/cadreprincipal.htm

The Council of Europe addressed the issue of privacy and data protection in its January 28, 1981, document titled *Convention for the Protection of Individuals with Regard to Automatic Processing of Personal Data*. As of 2002, twenty-nine of the member states in the Council of

Europe have ratified the document. It became effective October 1, 1985. The objective of this convention was to strengthen data protection, that is, the legal protection of individuals with regard to automatic processing of personal information relating to them. It was the first binding international instrument to protect the individual against abuses that may accompany collection and processing of personal data and which sought at the same time to regulate the trans-frontier flow of personal data.

In addition to providing guarantees in relation to collection and processing of personal data, it outlaws processing of "sensitive" data on a person's race, politics, health, religion, sexual life, criminal record, etc., in the absence of proper legal safeguards. The Convention also enshrines the individual's right to know that information is stored on him or her and, if necessary, to have it corrected.

Restriction of the rights in the Convention is only possible when overriding interests (state security, defense, etc.) are at stake. The Convention also imposes some restrictions on trans-border flows of personal data to nations where legal regulation does not provide equivalent protection. The Convention contains privacy and data protection provisions similar to the OECD. These are found online at the COE Web site.

European Union (EU)

http://europa.eu.int/comm/internal_market/en/dataprot/index.htm

The European Union's comprehensive privacy legislation, the *Directive on Data Protection* ("the Directive"), became effective October 25, 1998, three years after it was adopted. The Directive is intended to standardize protection of data privacy for European Union citizens, while allowing for the free flow of information between member states. The EU Directive prohibits the transfer of personally identifiable data to third countries that do not provide an "adequate" level of privacy protection.

Because the U.S. relies largely on sectoral (industry) and self-regulatory approaches to privacy protection (as opposed to legislative), many U.S. organizations were uncertain about the impact of the "adequacy" standard on personal data transfers from the EU to the U.S. To find ways to bridge differences in the approaches to privacy, the U.S. Department of Commerce, on behalf of the U.S. government, and the Directorate General XV of the European Commission engaged in a dialogue on privacy.

The result of that effort was that on July 26, 2000, the European Commission approved the U.S. Safe Harbor proposal. The agreement allows companies to abide voluntarily with a set of principles protecting data belonging to EU citizens. (It does not increase protections for U.S. citizens.) The

Commission approved this agreement despite a forceful resolution by the European Parliament adopted on July 5, 2000, that the agreement needed to be renegotiated to provide adequate protection.

Acknowledging the Parliament's criticisms, the Commission went ahead with the adoption of Safe Harbor with a promise to reopen negotiations on the arrangement if the remedies available to European citizens prove inadequate. EU member states were given 90 days to put the Commission's decision into effect; U.S. companies were permitted to join Safe Harbor starting November 1, 2000.

US/EU Safe Harbor Agreement
http://www.export.gov/safeharbor/

Organizations within the Safe Harbor have a presumption of adequacy; data transfers from any European Union country to them may continue. Organizations come within the Safe Harbor by self-certifying that they adhere to these privacy principles: notice, choice, onward transfer, security, data integrity, access, and enforcement, as defined below:

Notice

An organization must inform individuals about what types of personal information it collects about them, how it collects that information, the purposes for which it collects such information, the types of organizations to which it discloses the information, and the choices and means the organization offers individuals for limiting its use and disclosure. This notice must be provided in clear and conspicuous language that is readily understood and made available when individuals are first asked to provide personal information to the organization.

Choice

An organization must give individuals the opportunity to choose (opt-out choice) whether and how personal information they provide is used (where such use is unrelated to the use(s) for which they originally disclosed it). They must be provided with clear and conspicuous, readily available, and affordable mechanisms to exercise this option. For certain kinds of sensitive information, such as medical information, they must be given affirmative or explicit (opt-in) choice.

- Example 1 — Right to Object to Direct Marketing: The right to opt-out of additional uses means that the individuals must normally be given the opportunity to opt out of any marketing use of the data. Typically, the individuals are given separate opportunities to opt out of:
  - Receiving marketing materials, and
  - Receiving third-party marketing materials.

This can be broken down further by greater granularity, such as dividing the choice to receive company information into two or more choices: (1-a) receiving offers related to a specific product or service, and (1-b) receiving offers related to other company products or services, but these choices must be accurately reflected in the database and be retained if and when the data is transferred or merged into different systems.

- Example 2 — Third-party Transfers: Unless transferring the personal data to a third party is necessary to complete the specific transaction for which the data was provided, individuals should be given the opportunity to choose whether the data is shared with a third party. In either case, prior to transferring personal data to third parties, a company should require that the third party provide at least the same level of privacy protection as originally chosen by the individual. Whenever data is transferred to or shared with another system, the scope of permissible use and all customer preferences should be transferred as well.

Note that the individual's consent should be specific to the purpose or purposes for which the data is to be used and should be given following adequate disclosure as to those purposes. If data is collected for one purpose but subsequently used for another purpose, it will be necessary to obtain the consent of the individual to the new use of the data. If the individual has been given the opportunity to "opt out" of a particular use of the data and has not exercised that opportunity, disclosure has been made and consent will be considered given.

Onward Transfer

Individuals must be given the opportunity to choose whether and how a third party uses the personal information they provide (when such use is unrelated to the use(s) for which the individual originally disclosed it). When transferring personal information to third parties, an organization must require that third parties provide at least the same level of privacy protection as originally chosen by the individual. For certain kinds of sensitive information, such as medical information, individuals must be given "opt-in" choice.

Security

Organizations creating, maintaining, using, or disseminating records of personal information must take reasonable measures to assure its reliability for its intended use and must take reasonable precautions to protect it from loss, misuse, unauthorized access or disclosure, alteration, or destruction.

Data Integrity

An organization must keep personal data relevant to the purposes for which it has been gathered only, consistent with the principles of notice and choice. To the extent necessary for those purposes, the data should be accurate, complete, and current.

Access

Individuals must have reasonable access to information about them derived from non-public records that an organization holds, and be able to correct or amend that information when it is inaccurate. Reasonableness of access depends on the nature and sensitivity of the information collected and its intended uses. For instance, access must be provided to an individual where the information in question is sensitive or used for substantive decision-making purposes that affect that individual.

Enforcement

Effective privacy protection must include mechanisms for assuring compliance with the principles, recourse for individuals, and consequences for the organization when the principles are not followed. At a minimum, such mechanisms must include:

- Readily available and affordable independent recourse mechanisms by which individuals' complaints and disputes can be resolved.

- Systems for verifying that attestations and assertions businesses make about their privacy practices are true, and privacy practices have been implemented as presented.

- Obligations to remedy problems arising out of and consequences for organizations announcing adoption of these principles and failing to comply with them. Sanctions must be sufficient to ensure compliance by organizations and must provide individuals the means for enforcement.

It is important to bear in mind that the exceptions listed in Article 26 of the EU Directive are still applicable to all data transfers from the European Union to the U.S. Those include transfers to third countries where:

1. An individual has given unambiguous consent;
2. The transfer is necessary to complete a contract between the individual and the organization, or a contract is concluded in the interest of the individual between the organization and a third party;

3. The transfer is necessary or legally required on important public interest grounds or for legal actions;
4. The transfer is necessary to protect the vital interests of the individual; or
5. The data comes directly from public records.

Safe Harbor, like most data protection guidelines, laws, and regulations, applies to online and offline data (e.g., data collected via telephone, fax, registration cards, etc.).

Who is Affected by Safe Harbor

Any company that collects data from EU citizens and transfers it into the U.S. is potentially subject to Safe Harbor. Those subject to Safe Harbor compliance must do so or make alternative arrangements that meet adequacy requirements for data transfers from the EU. If a company is not registered for Safe Harbor, and requires data flows from the EU, it is required to establish contract terms that meet EU data protection/Safe Harbor requirements.

For most U.S. companies that do business in the EU with multiple partners, vendors, suppliers, and customers, this will prove an inefficient solution due to the costly process needed to manage and administer multiple agreements. In addition, these agreements might vary between countries due to specific laws that might have to be considered.

United Nations (UN)
http://www.un.org/ and *http://europa.eu.int/comm/internal_market/en/dataprot/inter/un.htm*

The General Assembly of the UN adopted *Guidelines Concerning Computerized Data Files* on December 14, 1990. Adoption in law was left to each member state. The principles contained within the Guidelines are:

1. Principle of Lawfulness and Fairness — Information about persons should not be collected or processed in unfair or unlawful ways, nor should it be used for ends contrary to the purposes and principles of the Charter of the United Nations.

2. Principle of Accuracy — Persons responsible for the compilation of files or those responsible for keeping them have an obligation to conduct regular checks on the accuracy and relevance of the data recorded and to ensure that they are kept as complete as possible in order to avoid errors of omission, and that they are kept up to date regularly or when the information contained in a file is used, as long as they are being processed.

3. Principle of the Purpose-Specification — The purpose which a file is to serve and its utilization in terms of that purpose should be specified, legitimate, and, when it is established, receive a certain amount of publicity or be brought to the attention of the person concerned, to make it possible subsequently to ensure that:
   - All the personal data collected and recorded remain relevant and adequate to the purposes so specified.
   - None of the said personal data is used or disclosed, except with consent of the person concerned, for purposes incompatible with those specified.
   - The period for which the personal data are kept does not exceed that which would enable the achievement of the purpose so specified.

4. Principle of Interested-person Access — Everyone who offers proof of identity has the right to know whether information concerning him is being processed and to obtain it in an intelligible form, without undue delay or expense, and to have appropriate rectification or erasures made in the case of unlawful, unnecessary, or inaccurate entries and, when it is being communicated, addressees. Provision should be made for a remedy, if need be, with the supervisory authority (specified in principle 8). The cost of any rectification shall be borne by the person responsible for the file. It is desirable that the provisions of this principle should apply to everyone, irrespective of nationality or place of residence.

5. Principle of Nondiscrimination — Subject to cases of exceptions restrictively envisaged under principle 6, data likely to give rise to unlawful or arbitrary discrimination, including information on racial or ethnic origin, color, sex life, political opinions, religious, philosophical and other beliefs as well as membership of an association or trade union, should not be compiled.

6. Power to Make Exceptions — Departures from principles 1 to 4 may be authorized only if they are necessary to protect national security, public order, public health or morality, as well as, inter alia, the rights and freedoms of others, especially people being persecuted (humanitarian clause) provided that such departures are expressly specified in a law or equivalent regulation promulgated in accordance with the internal legal system which expressly states their limits and sets forth appropriate safeguards. Exceptions to principle 5 relating to the prohibition of discrimination, in addition to being subject to the same safeguards as those prescribed for exceptions to principles 1 and 4, may be authorized only within the limits prescribed by the International Bill of Human Rights and the other relevant instruments in the field of protection of human rights and the prevention of discrimination.

7. Principle of Security — Appropriate measures should be taken to protect the files against both natural dangers, such as accidental loss or destruction, and human dangers, such as unauthorized access, fraudulent misuse of data, or contamination by computer viruses.

The Institute of Internal Auditors Research Foundation

8. Supervision and Sanctions — The law of every country shall designate the authority, which in accordance with its domestic legal system is to be responsible for supervising observance of the principles set forth above. This authority shall offer guarantees of impartiality, independence vis-à-vis persons or agencies responsible for processing and establishing data, and technical competence. In the event of violation of the provisions of the national law implementing the aforementioned principles, criminal or other penalties should be envisaged together with the appropriate individual remedies.

9. Trans-border Data Flows — When the legislation of two or more countries concerned by a trans-border data flow offers comparable safeguards for the protection of privacy, information should be able to circulate as freely as inside each of the territories concerned. If there are no reciprocal safeguards, limitations on such circulation may not be imposed unduly and only insofar as the protection of privacy demands.

10. Field of Application — The present principles should be made applicable, in the first instance, to all public and private computerized files as well as, by means of optional extension and subject to appropriate adjustments, to manual files. Special provision, also optional, might be made to extend all or part of the principles to files on legal persons particularly when they contain some information on individuals.

Canada

On January 1, 2001, the Canadian Personal Information Protection and Electronic Documents Act went into effect. The law established rules that govern the collection, use, and disclosure of personal information by private sector entities. The law establishes Fair Information Practices, based on the Canadian Standards Association (CSA) International Privacy Code, for personal data collected by federally regulated private sector organizations.

Federally regulated sectors include telecommunications, finance, and transportation. In the three years following passage, the provisions of the Act will also apply to provincially regulated industries unless provinces enact laws providing a similar level of protection. Data transfers are handled through the use of contracts that guarantee third parties operate under the same privacy guidelines as the original recipient. The Office of the Privacy Commissioner of Canada enforces the Act. More information about the Canadian Personal Information Protection and Electronic Documents Act is available at: http://www.privcom.gc.ca/legislation/02_06_01_e.asp.

Unlike the US/EU Safe Harbor program, the Canadian Personal Information Protection and Electronic Documents Act does not cover personal business information, such as business address and business phone number.

U.S. Government Activity

The U.S. has legislated on the subject of privacy on an exception basis, often called sectoral or sector-specific. A baseline level of privacy protection for the U.S. citizen has not materialized in laws and regulations to date, although this is still evolving. Paragraphs below describe the major legislative actions that have occurred; however, the list cannot be considered complete, as numerous new or additional initiatives exist within the U.S. Congress and the individual states that are not included.

Fair Credit Reporting Act of 1970
http://www.ftc.gov/os/statutes/fcra.htm

FCRA governs the use and disclosure of information affecting an individual's creditworthiness. The purpose of the Act is twofold:

1. Ensure the accuracy and fairness of credit reporting. Congress' statement of purpose found that:
    -   The banking system is dependent upon fair and accurate credit reporting. Inaccurate credit reports directly impair the efficiency of the banking system, and unfair credit reporting methods undermine public confidence, which is essential to the continued functioning of the banking system.
    -   An elaborate mechanism has been developed for investigating and evaluating the credit worthiness, credit standing, credit capacity, character, and general reputation of consumers.
    -   Consumer reporting agencies have assumed a vital role in assembling and evaluating consumer credit and other information on consumers.
    -   There is a need to insure that consumer reporting agencies exercise their grave responsibilities with fairness, impartiality, and a respect for the consumer's right to privacy.

2. Require that consumer-reporting agencies employ reasonable procedures for meeting the needs of commerce for consumer credit, personnel, insurance, and other information in a manner that is fair and equitable to the consumer, with regard to the confidentiality, accuracy, relevancy, and proper utilization of such information in accordance with the requirements of this title.

FCRA continues to be amended, with significant amendments made by the Consumer Credit Reporting Reform Act of 1996, which was effective October 1, 1997.

Privacy Act of 1974
U.S. Department of Justice - http://www.usdoj.gov/foia/privstat.htm

Broadly stated, the purpose of the Privacy Act is to balance the government's need to maintain information about individuals with the rights of individuals to be protected against unwarranted invasions of privacy stemming from federal agencies' collection, maintenance, use, and disclosure of personal information about them.

The historic context of the Act is important to understanding its remedial purposes: In 1974, Congress was concerned with curbing the illegal surveillance and investigation of individuals by federal agencies that had been exposed during the Watergate scandal; it was also concerned with potential abuses presented by the government's increasing use of computers to store and retrieve personal data by means of a universal identifier, such as an individual's Social Security number.

The Act focuses on four basic policy objectives:

1. To restrict <u>disclosure</u> of personally identifiable records maintained by agencies.
2. To grant individuals increased rights of <u>access</u> to agency records maintained on themselves.
3. To grant individuals the right to seek <u>amendment</u> of agency records maintained on themselves upon a showing that the records are not accurate, relevant, timely, or complete.
4. To establish a code of "<u>fair information practices</u>" which requires agencies to comply with statutory norms for collection, maintenance, and dissemination of records.

The Act became effective on September 27, 1975. According to the Department of Justice source cited below, the Act's imprecise language, limited legislative history, and somewhat outdated regulatory guidelines have rendered it a difficult statute to decipher and apply. Moreover, even after 20 years of administrative and judicial analysis, numerous Privacy Act issues remain unresolved or unexplored.

Right to Financial Privacy Act of 1978
U.S. Department of Labor - http://www.dol.gov/dol/allcfr/Title_29/Part_19/toc.htm

The Act prohibits the government from accessing an individual's financial records except as provided for in the law (e.g., subpoena, search warrant, or summons). Individuals may be asked to consent to make their financial records available to the government. They may withhold consent, and consent is not required as a condition of doing business with any financial institution. If consent is given, it can be revoked in writing at any time before anything is disclosed. Furthermore, any consent given is effective for only three months, and your financial institution must keep a record of the instances in which it discloses your financial information.

Generally, a federal agency must give an individual advance notice of its request for their records explaining why the information is being sought and telling them how to object in court. The agency must send them copies of court documents to be prepared with instructions for filling them out.

In some circumstances, a federal agency may obtain financial information about an individual without advance notice or consent. In most of these cases, the agency is required to go to court to get permission to obtain such records without giving notice beforehand. In these instances, the court will make the government show that its investigation and request for records is proper. A federal agency that obtains an individual's financial records is prohibited from transferring them to another federal agency unless it certifies in writing that the transfer is proper and sends a notice to the individual that their records have been sent to another agency.

If a federal agency or financial institution violates the Right to Financial Privacy Act, an individual may sue for damages or seek compliance with the law. If the individual wins, they may have attorney's fees and costs repaid.

Cable TV Privacy Act of 1984

The purpose of CTVPA is to protect consumers from unauthorized collection and disclosure of personal information. The Act requires notice to consumers of the "nature and use" of information collected as well as the "nature and use" of any disclosure of personal information. It also requires prior written or electronic consent before a cable operator can collect personally identifiable information. In general, disclosure of such information is prohibited, requiring a cable operator to take steps to prevent unauthorized access to personally identifiable information collected.

There are exceptions to the collection and disclosure prohibitions. The Act permits collection of personally identifiable information if necessary to render a cable service or detect unauthorized reception of cable communications. It also allows disclosure if it is necessary to render cable or related service provided by the cable operator, or where disclosure is mandated pursuant to a court order, if the consumer is notified. Additionally, the CTVPA permits disclosure if the consumer failed to "opt out" when the cable operator provides the opportunity to prohibit or limit disclosure, and disclosure does not reveal transactional information of the consumer.

Cable operators must provide the subject access to the personally identifiable information collected. Information that the cable operator no longer requires for the purpose for which it was collected must be destroyed. In addition to any other remedies the consumer might have available, the CTVPA provides for civil remedies that include: (1) attorney's fees; (2) damages not less than $100 per day or $1,000 per violation whichever is greater; and (3) punitive damages.

Electronic Communication Privacy Act of 1986

http://policyworks.gov/policydocs/5.pdf

Electronic surveillance or wiretapping was first addressed by Title III of the Omnibus Crime Control and Safe Streets Act of 1968 after the Supreme Court determined that the use by FBI agents of electronic devices to listen to and record telephone conversations without a warrant constituted a violation of unreasonable search and seizure provisions established by the Fourth Amendment. ECPA was designed to expand Title III privacy protection to apply to a number of other electronic communications, such as radio paging devices, electronic mail, cellular telephones, private communication carriers, and computer transmissions. The Act:

1. Makes it illegal to intercept wire, oral, or electronic communications.
2. Requires communication providers to keep communications confidential in transmission and in storage.
3. Requires that stored data cannot be accessed without authorization.

The Act also identified specific situations and types of transmissions that would not be protected, most notably an employer's monitoring of employee electronic mail on the employer's system.

Computer Matching and Privacy Protection Act of 1988

http://www.usdoj.gov/04foia/1974compmatch.htm

The Computer Matching and Privacy Protection Act of 1988 amended the Privacy Act to add several new provisions with procedural requirements for agencies to follow when engaging in computer-matching activities; to provide matching subjects with opportunities to receive notice and to refute adverse information before having a benefit denied or terminated; and require that agencies engaged in matching activities establish Data Protection Boards to oversee those activities.

These provisions became effective on December 31, 1989. Subsequently, Congress enacted the Computer Matching and Privacy Protection Amendments of 1990, which further clarify the due process provisions found in subsection (p).

Video Privacy Protection Act of 1988

This Act forbids disclosure of the rental records of customers without their express consent. A videotape service provider who knowingly discloses, to any person, personally identifiable information concerning any consumer of such provider shall be liable to the aggrieved person for the relief provided elsewhere in the law. The law prevents video renters from selling consumer information to direct marketers.

The Act is also known as the "Bork Law." In 1987, the Democrats attacked President Ronald Reagan's choice for U.S. Supreme Court Justice — Robert Bork — by subpoena of his video rental records. His opponents sought to prevent his appointment by attacking his reputation and they were hopeful that his choices in video rentals would prove embarrassing.

Communications Assistance to Law Enforcement Act of 1994

The purpose of CALEA is to make clear a telecommunications carrier's duty to cooperate in the interception of communications for law enforcement purposes, and for other purposes. CALEA reportedly makes it mandatory for all companies developing telephone switching, cellular, and satellite communications technologies to build in surveillance capabilities.

Health Insurance Portability and Accountability Act of 1996
U.S. Department of Health and Human Services - http://www.hhs.gov/ocr/hipaa/

HIPAA is a national privacy bill designed to set policies for the legal use of identifiable health information, including access to personal medical information, an individual's rights regarding his or her information, and what constitutes inappropriate access. The final rule adopting HIPAA standards for the security of electronic health information was published in the Federal Register on February 20, 2003. This final rule specifies a series of administrative, technical, and physical security procedures for covered entities to use to assure the confidentiality of electronic protected health information. The standards are delineated into either required or addressable implementation specifications.

HIPAA's Administrative Simplification provision is composed of four parts, each of which have generated a variety of rules and standards. The four parts of Administrative Simplification are:

1. **Electronic Health Transactions Standards.** The Transactions Rule was published on August 17, 2000. The compliance date is October 16, 2002.
2. **Unique Identifiers.**
3. **Security & Electronic Signature Standards.**
4. **Privacy & Confidentiality Standards.** The Privacy Rule was published on December 28, 2000, but due to an error, did not become effective until April 14, 2001. Compliance is required on April 14, 2003.

As an organization prepares to develop its enterprise-wide security program, it should keep in mind that the privacy standards:

- Limit the non-consensual use and release of private health information.

- Give patients new rights to access their medical records and to know who else has accessed them.

- Restrict most disclosure of health information to the minimum needed for the intended purpose.

- Establish new criminal and civil sanctions for improper use or disclosure. Specifically, HIPAA calls fines up to $25K for multiple violations of the same standard in a calendar year and fines up to $250K and/or imprisonment up to 10 years for knowing misuse of individually identifiable health information.

- Establish new requirements for access to records by researchers and others.

The new regulation reflects the following five principles:

- **Consumer Control:** The regulation provides consumers with critical new rights to control the release of their medical information.

- **Boundaries:** With few exceptions, an individual's health-care information should be used for health purposes only, including treatment and payment.

- **Accountability:** Under HIPAA, for the first time, there will be specific federal penalties if a patient's right to privacy is violated.

- **Public Responsibility:** The new standards reflect the need to balance privacy protections with the public responsibility to support such national priorities as protecting public health, conducting medical research, improving the quality of care, and fighting health care fraud and abuse.

- **Security:** It is the responsibility of organizations that are entrusted with health information to protect it against deliberate or inadvertent misuse or disclosure.

Children's Online Privacy Protection Act of 1998
http://www.ftc.gov/os/1999/9910/64fr59888.pdf

COPPA, effective April 21, 2000, applies to the online collection of personal information from children under 13. The law spells out what a Web site operator must include in a privacy policy, when and how to seek verifiable consent from a parent, and what responsibilities an operator has to protect children's privacy and safety online. Operators of commercial Web sites or online services directed to children under 13 that collect personal information must comply, plus operators of a general audience Web site that have actual knowledge that they are collecting personal information from children.

The Federal Trade Commission (FTC) can bring enforcement actions and impose civil penalties for violations of the Rule in the same manner as for other Rules under the FTC Act. The Commission also retains authority under Section 5 of the FTC Act to examine information practices for deception and unfairness, including those in use before the Rule's effective date. The FTC believes it is a deceptive practice under Section 5 to represent that a Web site is collecting personally identifying information from a child for one reason (say, to earn points to redeem a premium) when the information will be used for another reason that a parent would find material — and when the Web site does not disclose the other reason clearly or prominently. They also contend that it is likely to be an unfair practice in violation of Section 5 to collect personally identifying information from a child, such as an e-mail address, home address, or phone number, and disclose that information to a third party without giving parents adequate notice and a chance to control the collection and use of the information.

For more information about COPPA, see http://www.ftc.gov/opa/1999/9910/childfinal.htm. The Direct Marketing Association (DMA) offers a privacy policy generator for Web sites that must comply with COPPA. See http://www.the-dma.org/library/privacy/childrensppg.shtml

Deceptive Mail Prevention and Enforcement Act of 1999
http://frwebgate.access.gpo.gov/cgi-bin/getdoc.cgi?dbname=106_cong_bills&docid =f:s335enr.txt.pdf

The Act took effect on April 12, 2000. It covers "sweepstakes mailings, skill contests, facsimile checks, and mailings made to resemble government documents." The so-called "Sweepstakes Law" gives considerable new authority to the U.S. Postal Service, granting it subpoena power, nationwide "stop mail" authority, and the ability to impose severe civil penalties. The Act also requires mailers of sweepstakes and skill contests to establish a name removal notification system whereby individuals can request removal from mailing lists used for sweepstakes and contests. Finally, the Act establishes strong financial penalties for sending mailings that violate the Act. For more information, see: http://www.the-dma.org/library/guidelines/sweepstakesdosdonts.shtml

Financial Services Modernization Act of 1999
http://www.ftc.gov/privacy/glbact/

The Financial Services Modernization Act, also known as the Gramm Leach Bliley Act or GLB, was passed November 12, 1999, effective November 13, 2000, with required compliance by July 1, 2001. Seven federal agencies issued regulations implementing the privacy provisions of the Act. Title V of GLB provides the first ever regulation of privacy of personal financial information in the private sector.

Financial institutions, defined as any enterprise engaged in "financial activities" (including insurance companies), must establish written policies for protection of customer information. Such policies are required to:

- Assure the security and confidentiality of nonpublic personal information.
- Protect against threats to its integrity or security.
- Protect against unauthorized access or use.

The policies should be based on the Standards for Safeguarding Customer Information as outlined in the Federal Register, Volume 66, No. 22/February 1, 2002/Rules and Regulations. This section also discusses the development and implementation of the information security program. See: http://www.fdic.gov/regulations/laws/federal/01Part2.pdf

Under the GLB Act, organizations must provide initial and yearly notices to customers on personal information gathered and its use. The GLB Act is applicable to the privacy of individuals only and is not applicable to "business privacy." The following items must be included in the privacy notice:

- Categories of personal information your company collects.

- Categories of personal information you disclose.

- Categories of affiliates and nonaffiliated third parties to whom you disclose the information.

- An explanation of the right to opt out of disclosures to nonaffiliated third parties.

- A description of the kind of disclosures to nonaffiliated parties that are exceptions to the rules and don't give the consumer the right to opt out.

- An explanation of the ability to opt out of disclosures of information among affiliates under the Fair Credit Reporting Act (FCRA).

- If your company discloses information to third parties, a separate statement of the categories of information disclosed and the categories of third parties to whom the information will be disclosed, must be included.

- A description of your confidentiality and security policies and practices.

- Categories of personal information about former customers disclosed and to whom such information was disclosed.

Customers must have the ability to "opt out," that is to deny the institution permission to share information with unaffiliated third parties. Sharing among affiliates is permitted regardless of customer consent. Important exceptions to the opt-out (permitting the financial institution to share consumer information with third parties) include:

1. Joint marketing agreements complying with federal policy regulations.
2. Enforcement of a transaction requested by the customer (this includes securitization or secondary market sales).
3. Protecting the institution's records against fraud.
4. Providing information to rating agencies, insurance agencies, or similar entities evaluating the financial condition or performance of the institution.

State insurance regulators have responsibility to enforce federal privacy regulations as they pertain to insurers. If a state authority fails to adopt regulations to carry out this responsibility, the state will not be eligible to override the federally prescribed customer protection regulators pertaining to bank-affiliated insurance sales under Title III. The Act requires compliance of the following:

- Financial institutions
- Insurance companies
- Stock exchanges and brokerages
- Loan brokers
- Loan servicers
- Real or personal property leasing companies (brokers, agents, advisors, and lessors) if they do not operate, maintain, or repair the property
- Real or personal property appraisers
- Check guaranty companies
- Collection agencies
- Credit bureaus
- Real estate settlement services

- Providers of financial or investment advisory activities (tax planners, tax preparers, and instructors of financial management)
- Management consulting and counseling services (including financial career counseling)
- Courier services that carry financial instruments
- Check printers
- Sellers of money orders, savings bonds, traveler's checks
- Financial data processing and transmission services, facilities, databases, etc.

U.S. Congress

The Privacy issue is bipartisan. A bipartisan source of privacy discussions is the Congressional Internet Caucus, whose purpose is to educate Congress and the public about Internet-related policy issues. See www.netcaucus.org and search the Issues section for privacy. There are numerous proposed laws in both the House of Representatives and Senate. To see current activity of both houses of Congress, go to www.senate.gov/ and use the Bill Search function under Legislation & Records to search for the word "privacy" or go directly to http://thomas.loc.gov/ and make the same search. A recent search produced a list of 50 bills.

Federal Trade Commission
http://www.ftc.gov/privacy

The Federal Trade Commission's primary legislative mandate is to enforce the Federal Trade Commission Act, which prohibits unfair methods of competition and unfair or deceptive acts or practices in or affecting commerce. Commerce on the Internet falls within the scope of this statutory mandate. The FTC's goal has been to understand this new marketplace and its information practices, and assess the impact of these practices on consumers. For some time, the FTC encouraged industry self-regulation as the preferred approach to protecting consumer privacy online.

In a reversal of FTC reports to Congress in 1998 and 1999 that advocated self-regulation over legislation, the FTC began recommending a legislative approach in a report to Congress on May 22, 2000, which concluded that self-regulation is not enough to cope with online privacy violations. In calling for Congress to pass privacy legislation, the FTC provided evidence that its "sweep" of Web sites' privacy policies and tests of compliance with fair information practices indicated that self-regulation was not working sufficiently to stave off privacy regulation.

In the 2000 sweeps, the commission examined 100 of the busiest sites and a random sample of 335 other sites to see how many provided notice, choice, access, and security. It found great improvement since the previous report, but still reported levels of compliance far too low to permit worry-free surfing by consumers. Even on the least controversial measures — notice and choice — only 41 percent of the random sample and 60 percent of the most popular sites implemented both.

The Report's proposal for an opt-out standard means that calls for opt-in rules will weaken, while the FTC's focus on access will place the issue front and center. By centering the debate on its four criteria — and not the broader Organization for Economic Cooperation and Development (OECD) guidelines favored by privacy advocates — the report ensures that even after the 2001 round of legislation, the disconnect between U.S. and European privacy standards will continue.

The FTC has been active in efforts to become *the* privacy regulator. For example, it:

- Convened an advisory panel to help the agency craft fair information practices for governing online privacy access and security. Members of the panel represented both industry and privacy advocates, and focused on consumers' "access" to online personal information and the "security" of such information.
- Drafted the privacy regulations in Title V of the GLB Act.
- Approved the self-regulatory principles developed by the Network Advertising Initiative.

The Safe Harbor principles, principally negotiated by the Department of Commerce with the EU, mandate that the U.S. Federal Trade Commission (FTC) expedite complaints by EU citizens about how their data was handled in the U.S., thus processing them faster than complaints from U.S. citizens.

Department of Commerce
http://www.ita.doc.gov/td/ecom/menu.html

The Department of Commerce is deeply involved in defining the implications of foreign policy on U.S. businesses. The DOC has worked on behalf of U.S. entities to encourage industry to establish self-regulatory programs and technology solutions to protect privacy, particularly, but not exclusively, in the online environment. The hope is that self-regulation through voluntary programs will be sufficient to establish "adequate" levels of protection, thus providing U.S. companies with insulation or "Safe Harbor" from the prohibitions of the EU Directive, as long as they live up to their publicized privacy policies. The DOC has worked with the EU on this issue for some time and drafted an important paper on the subject titled "The Elements for Effective Privacy Protection."

Through the DOC Task Force on Electronic Commerce, International Trade Administration, the Safe Harbor was approved by the EC Parliament and finalized July 21, 2000. U.S. companies can cooperate in one of four ways:

1. By reporting to a data authority in Europe
2. By agreeing to be monitored by U.S. authorities
3. By joining a self-regulatory body, monitored by the FTC
4. By agreeing to rules set by a European panel of data privacy officials

The DOC will keep a list of industry self-regulators, providing oversight to ensure they comply with privacy rules. Companies wishing to adhere to the principles sign up with the DOC and are placed on a database available to the public over the Internet. Failure to comply with Safe Harbor is considered a deceptive business practice and a prosecutable offense. Organizations doing so subject themselves to investigation by the Department of Justice, state attorneys general, and the FTC.

CHAPTER 3
EFFECTIVE PRACTICES AND THE AUDITOR'S ROLE IN PRIVACY

Introduction

One of the problems facing today's organizations is addressing the growing concern about privacy practices. Deciding just what to do and how is an issue. An independent study showed that the majority of organizations with privacy policies posted on their Web sites were not in compliance with them. Perhaps that sort of information, anecdotal and otherwise, is one of the reasons that within the U.S., the Federal Trade Commission (FTC) recently announced it would not push for new laws, but rather enforcement of the ones in place.

To compound the issue, the need to deal effectively with globalization, with its different and sometimes conflicting requirements, and pressure from the outside to share information about security lapses make it even more difficult for an organization to respond. Yet, there are ways to assess organizational effectiveness based on awareness, maturity, and compliance. The role of the board of directors and the "tone at the top" are key aspects.

The objective of this chapter is to discuss effective practices for managing the risks associated with privacy. It also provides guidance on how an organization can achieve privacy objectives and the role the auditor should have in the process. One useful idea is a Capability Maturity Model (CMM) for privacy, much like the model published by the Software Engineering Institute (SEI) to characterize the maturity of organizations based on their practices in software development. This chapter presents a conceptual framework loosely based on the original CMM. Assessing maturity can help management and auditors see where they are within a spectrum and respond accordingly. Last, the chapter provides lessons learned from recent privacy debacles.

Oversight Role

One of the basics is awareness of the issues. Starting with its directors, people throughout the organization need to know the issues and what to do. The following questions highlight issues surrounding privacy with which boards of directors should be aware:

- Has the organization selected an individual or created a specific position responsible for privacy, such as a chief privacy officer, and provided resources?

- Does the organization operate in any areas of the world where it is required to comply with privacy laws and regulations protecting the rights of citizens in those jurisdictions?

- Does the organization have appropriate privacy, information security and protection, and risk management processes in place?

- Is the organization subject to potential fines and penalties for failure to comply with laws and regulations such as:
  - U.S. Health Insurance Portability and Accountability Act (HIPAA),
  - U.S. Gramm-Leach-Bliley Financial Services Modernization Act (GLB),
  - U.S. Children's Online Privacy Protection Act (COPPA),
  - EU Data Directive/U.S. DoC Safe Harbor agreement, or the like?

- If a privacy debacle were to occur, could the resulting loss of customer trust damage the organization's market valuation, revenue stream, or public image?

- Does the organization's business model rely substantially on establishing trust with users regarding protection of their personally identifying information (PII) before success can be achieved or to fuel the growth of the customer base?

- What does the organization stand to gain by addressing the privacy concerns of online users, or stand to lose by not addressing the privacy concerns of online users?

- Does the organization have a published privacy policy that states clearly their position on all of the generally accepted fair information practices?

- What steps does the organization take to ensure that the entire organization is aware of and compliant with their policy?

- Does the organization treat the PII collected from individuals with the same high standard regardless of whether it is collected offline or online, or subject to laws and regulations versus not?

The Role of the Chief Privacy Officer (CPO)

Characteristics and responsibilities of the CPO in an organization include:

- Organize and coordinate the organization's privacy task force or privacy committee.
- Commission or conduct a privacy risk assessment and remedy all findings.

- Monitor performance in the privacy environment.
- Develop or facilitate the development of the privacy policy and procedures.
- Monitor laws and regulations.
- Review new products for privacy implications that might indicate privacy of users would be violated in fact or in appearance.
- Support/deliver employee privacy training, as well as that for the press and government.
- Communicate the actions taken by the organization to address concerns.
- Monitor consumer watchdog groups.
- Manage privacy dispute resolution process.
- Speak for the organization and prepare executives for testimony when you cannot speak.
- Conduct regular privacy audits; search out and expose any internal practices that are not consistent with the privacy policy.
- Report to top management on privacy and solicit support for improvements.
- Promote compliance with the organization's privacy policy on the part of affiliates in receipt of personally identifying information.
- Persuade the entire organization to buy into respecting the privacy of users.

Compiled from *Rise of the Chief Privacy Officer*, presentation by Dr. Alan Westin, Professor of Public Law and Government Emeritus at Columbia University, September 2000.

Enabling Technologies for Privacy

There are many different technology options for privacy program management on both the business and consumer sides. They fall into the following categories:

- Privacy preference disclosure programs
- Privacy rights management programs
- Privacy filtering solutions
- Anonymizer solutions

The Auditor's Role in Privacy

The privacy issue and protection of PII provide a compelling platform for auditors to perform information security reviews. Following the PII trail from collection/input, through processing, use, storage, and dissemination/output, and finally destruction can reveal where control points exist through multiple layers, from business to IT infrastructure. Mitigating IT exposures around privacy may provide opportunities to engage in more extensive collaboration with the audit customer to develop appropriate technology controls over vulnerabilities identified. This in turn can allow auditors to build credibility and competence in reviewing information technology controls, and expand and fortify the information security assurance program.

Reviewing information technology and security controls is difficult and can be quite costly in a distributed, networked IT environment of diverse technology platforms and integrated processes and systems. Auditors often find themselves in the position of having to sell their clients, internal or external, on the value of an information security audit. When there is little appreciation of the need or understanding of the sheer complexity of the task, development of the audit scope and objectives is hard at best. Being able to present the issue clearly, with potential solutions at the end of the process — rather than just problems — is a positive skill auditors may learn and employ.

External Audit's Role

Damage to an organization's reputation can have dramatic and serious financial repercussions. News spreads rapidly in the interconnected world, and such damage can affect the ability of the entity to continue as a going concern, raise capital in the markets, generate profits from sales, and sustain a viable workforce to manufacture, sell, and service products. The risk of improperly disclosing PII to external parties can also result in civil and criminal penalties that carry brand and reputation damage as unintended consequences.

While the role of external auditors in relation to privacy is still evolving, they can help the board and management understand the inherent risks involved in not adequately protecting employee, customer, and trading partner private information, and potential consequences. External audit may have a role in assessing the impact that absence of privacy practices may have on the overall financial and related operational risk profile an organization presents. This can ultimately affect inherent risk and the successful completion of an annual audit.

Internal Audit's Role

Internal audit can have a significant role in helping the enterprise establish and achieve privacy objectives. In some cases, internal audit may be the sole function that facilitates the initial awareness and establishment of privacy objectives to help get an organization's privacy program off the ground. As discussed below, internal audit can engage in a number of activities to ensure that sound privacy policies are in place, and practices are established and functioning effectively.

Maturity of Privacy Practices

One of the leading practices concepts is developing an understanding of where an organization is in the privacy "life cycle." Such knowledge will help auditors develop an approach to evaluate current privacy controls, and assist in developing an appropriate privacy strategy, policy, and deployment of privacy practices and controls across the organization.

A current problem is the desire of many to come to a full-blown solution immediately, when the organization is just not ready for it. Using a Capability Maturity Model (CMM) for privacy is loosely based on the conceptual framework of the model originally published by the Software Engineering Institute (SEI) to characterize software development maturity. The idea is that there are five levels of maturity, and organizations must address issues at each level before moving up.

Process and system improvements in managing privacy effectively have three basic activities:

(1) Measuring the maturity of the current process
(2) Determining priorities for improvement
(3) Implementing and monitoring the improvement plan

The internal auditor can develop strategic, independent facilitation and evaluation roles in all of these activities. The following areas outline the five levels of maturity:

Level 1 – Initial

As in the SEI model, activities at this stage are ad hoc. The organization has no defined policies, rules, or procedures to direct privacy activities across the organization. Departmental or individual activity may be underway, but activities are not strategic or coordinated. There is a lack of teamwork and commitment, similar processes may be redundant across the organization, and people may be frustrated (people who care and are committed meet with resistance due to a number of factors, including lack of awareness, other priorities, or lack of performance objectives in this area). At this level, the primary areas the auditor can influence are:

- Senior management commitment.
- Measuring the maturity of the current process.
- Privacy framework development.
- Policy development.
- Development of guiding principles.
- Awareness.

Level 2 – Repeatable

At this stage, the organization has a defined privacy policy and some level of demonstrated senior management commitment to addressing privacy requirements and issues. There is general awareness and commitment across the organization to meet the organization's privacy commitments. Specific plans are developing in high-risk areas, and people are aware and generally engaged. At this level, auditors can engage in the following areas:

- Privacy risk assessment across the organization:
  - Risk assessments should consider both the operational areas of the organization where personal information is collected, used, stored, and disseminated (for marketing, product registration/warranty purposes, for instance), or where products and/or services have potential privacy risks due to the manner in which those products and/or services use personal information.

  - Privacy risk assessments should consider internal risk, including collection, use, storage, or dissemination of personal employee information for human resource, health, benefits, and other purposes.

  - Risk assessments should consider third-party partners, vendors, affiliates, and others, who manage information on an organization's behalf, or where there are associations that may implicate the primary organization (e.g., primary organization hosts a Web site of a third-party affiliate). This relates to the primary and secondary uses of data discussed in the Privacy Legislation chapter.

  - Risk assessments should consider the visibility or profile of the product or service collecting or using the information to better understand the level of external risk.

  - Risk assessments should consider legal factors where the product or service is local to a specific country.

- Departmental or functional privacy risk assessments

- Establishing a privacy function and privacy officer for the organization

- Establishing/influencing a privacy task force

- Development/refinement and completeness of policy

- Compliance audits and reviews that focus on consistency of privacy policy, privacy statements, and functional approach for complying in specific areas

Level 3 – Defined

At this stage, the organization has demonstrated senior management commitment, complete privacy policy, and privacy organization and leadership is in place (possibly including a CPO). Risk assessments have been performed, priorities are established, resources allocated accordingly, and activities to coordinate and deploy effective, consistent privacy controls across the organization are underway. At this level, auditors can engage in the following areas:

- Review effectiveness of privacy policies, CPO activities, and deployment of privacy practices and controls across the organization.

- Perform compliance audits, including assessing practices, processes and controls around privacy policy, statements, and processes, data protection requirements and mechanisms, and related information security effectiveness.
    - As discussed later in the audit program section, comprehensive audits address privacy practices and controls at several levels ranging from the business level (policy, statements, education/awareness programs, and process around managing privacy), to online and offline processes, application and database level controls, and IT infrastructure and network level controls.
    - Effective privacy controls require tight integration between policy, processes, systems, and organizational functions (e.g., legal, HR, corporate privacy group, privacy task force, etc.). A comprehensive review will determine effectiveness and level of integration of privacy controls within these components.

- To the extent an organization has privacy considerations related directly to their products or services (e.g., software product in a technology organization), there are opportunities to evaluate how that product or service collects and manages personal information. Depending on the nature of the product, such as software or other technical products, the review may require very specialized or technical skills to determine and evaluate the effectiveness of privacy controls.

- Assist the privacy group in deploying surveys or self-assessments to determine the state of privacy. A control self-assessment framework might be an effective vehicle for supplementing privacy group activities, or for expanding the reach of a small or resource constrained privacy function.

Level 4 – Managed

The organization has reached a consistently effective level of maturity in managing privacy requirements and issues across the organization. Privacy requirements and considerations have been woven into the fabric of the organization, including consideration of privacy requirements early in process and system development, as well as meeting privacy requirements in existing processes and systems. While a dedicated privacy function still exists (e.g., CPO, privacy group), privacy is integrated into operational and products/services job functions, and performance objectives are established to meet privacy requirements. Monitoring of privacy effectiveness occurs at the organization level as well as within given functions; periodic reviews/audits occur based on risk assessment with results that privacy controls and processes are operating effectively and consistently. At this level, auditors can engage in the following areas:

- Refine and continue activities specified at Level 3.
- Review policies and standards for completeness and potential effectiveness against effective practices, emerging legislation, and specific practices in given countries in which the organization does business.

Level 5 – Optimizing

Level 5 organizations use practices evolved in Levels 1 through 4 to continually monitor and improve the effectiveness and quality of privacy policies, practices, and controls. No change is introduced into a new or existing process or system without being scrutinized by appropriate parties for privacy risks, opportunities, and activities to support privacy requirements. Additional resources are allocated to achieve privacy objectives in current and developing processes or systems, and there is a high level of organizational, functional, and systems integration to meet privacy objectives, as well as teamwork among cross-functional groups.

There is a great sense of pride and ownership across teams for deploying an effective privacy architecture and process framework across the organization. A relatively small number of organizations will achieve this level in the near future due to the significant organizational and operational challenges that must be overcome in Levels 1 through 4. At this level, auditors can engage through further refinement of audit, facilitation, and review activities.

Privacy Audit Assurance Program

The framework around privacy audit assurance is made up of a set of audit activities and methodologies to facilitate, influence, and assess an organization's privacy program. Outside of core privacy audits, the internal audit group can engage in facilitation activities as described above. The privacy audit assurance program is core to the operational level of this framework.

There are many types of reviews and approaches that may be considered to achieve certain objectives. These will encompass various components of the audit program. Some of the potential audit projects include:

- Enterprise and Privacy Policy Assessment.
- Facilitate Development of Privacy Program.
- Employee Privacy Policy and Data Protection Assessment.
- Enterprise Privacy and Network Security Capability Assessment.
- Network Risk, Security, and Architecture Assessment.
- Review of Enterprise Data Protection and Intrusion Monitoring Capabilities.
- Review of Enterprise Data Classification, Data Retention, Data Archiving, and Disposition Activities.
- E-Commerce Privacy Assessment.

Levels of Privacy Assessments

There are two general levels of assessment that can be performed: breadth and depth, which, as their names indicate, have different coverage and focus. Both can be broken down into smaller units so the auditor can provide assurance around a specific component. For instance, a breadth assessment could focus on the consistency and effectiveness of privacy statements across a large number of Web pages or sites. A depth assessment could focus on one aspect of the vertical layer, such as security around the marketing database.

Breadth Assessments

Breadth assessments provide an opportunity to develop a broad perspective and analysis across a number of related functions, processes, activities, and systems. Generally, this type of assessment can identify all of the activities and privacy control points related to a common set of PII collection and management functions.

For instance, an organization may be engaged in collecting product or warranty registration information via a combination of Web site, customer service phone support, and faxes. Data from each of these activities is entered through different applications, stored in different places, and aggregated in a back-end marketing database. Information is extracted from this database into a master customer database maintained by an entirely different function. It is important to note that these activities relate to both online and offline data.

In this example, there are numerous privacy risks and potential control points where the auditor might provide assessment and risk analysis. Areas such as policy, privacy statements, Web applications, telephone applications, back-end databases, transfers of data, uploads from remote locations, etc. should all be considered.

Breadth assessments are more conducive to higher-level risk assessments. The number of activities and systems that are included preclude detailed process, application, security, and information technology architecture reviews.

Depth Assessments

A depth assessment is a vertical, detailed audit approach to a specific business function and related processes, activities, and systems. An approach is developed to evaluate the business control environment, privacy policies and statements, applications used to collect, process, or store data, infrastructure components that the applications and files rely on, network and operating system configuration controls, IT operations processes, and so forth.

The greater level of detail means more focus on a specific function. A depth assessment can provide a complete assessment of risks and controls to understand the integrity of privacy management within a given business unit or function.

Audit Facilitation Opportunities

In some ways, privacy is like the Year 2000 issue. For many, the issue will span a large number of businesses, processes, activities, and systems. There may be constrained or no dedicated resources addressing privacy concerns, and the prospect of taking this on may be intimidating or its sheer complexity makes it appear to be an impossible task.

Control self-assessment can provide an opportunity to leverage audit knowledge across a broad set of businesses or areas of the organization. It might be done in support of a corporate privacy group or CPO, or as a business facilitation effort. One approach is to develop a privacy audit program that can be deployed into the organization's businesses and functions, and leverage personnel in those areas to execute the programs with or without internal audit assistance. A Web-based system where audit programs can be deployed and results consolidated, reviewed, and compared might be ideal in leveraging limited resources to help address a very high-risk issue.

CHAPTER 4
PRIVACY AUDIT PROGRAM

This chapter contains an overall framework and sample audit program to address privacy within an organization. Specific programs will depend on many factors, including how mature the organization is in privacy practice, skill sets in the audit group, resources available for technical assistance, and so forth.

The framework and program assume the existence of organization Web sites or other online systems that potentially collect personally identifying information (PII). They also assume appropriate research has been performed with internal and external resources, especially in-house counsel, to determine the exact nature of laws and regulations, and other standards and practices applicable to the organization and the countries in which it does business.

Outline of Program Objectives

Business Environment

- Understand privacy regulations, legislation, agreements, etc. applicable to your organization.
- Evaluate the online business and related applications to develop audit scope and framework.
- Evaluate the site/application to develop a framework for reviewing compliance with stated privacy policies.

Control Environment

- Evaluate the overall internal control environment to determine the need for ongoing privacy compliance. More favorable control environments may indicate a lower risk of privacy noncompliance.
- Evaluate privacy awareness.

Privacy Policy/Statement

- Assess your privacy policy for compliance with legislation, regulation, agreements, culture, ethics, business objectives, etc.
- Evaluate the effectiveness of the privacy policies and practices in place.

Privacy Policy/Statement — Content

- Determine whether the consumer has been notified about what information is collected, who is collecting the information (the organization or an outside third party), the intended use of the information collected, and whether the information will be used for secondary purposes.
- Determine whether the site or business unit application shares information with outside third parties. This includes gaining an understanding of whether the consumer is notified of the information shared with these third parties, the third parties' intended use of the information received, and the type and frequency of communications that they should expect to receive from third parties in the future.
- Determine how the site securely collects and stores information collected from consumers, the physical location where information collected is being stored, and whether consumers are notified of information storage processes and procedures.
- Determine whether the consumer has the option to (1) access their information collected by the organization to update or edit this information; (2) access their information to remove it; (3) request that the organization or a third party remove their information from the organization's systems; and (4) receive assurance that their request has been honored.
- Determine whether data collected are relevant and not excessive in relation to the purpose or purposes for which they are collected.
- Determine whether the consumer has been given the choice to opt-in or opt-out of receiving additional information or solicitations from the organization or related third parties, and whether this is adequately addressed in the underlying system architecture to honor these choices.

General Security Controls

- Determine whether system and application changes are being properly authorized, tested, and promoted into production.
- Identify within a framework of authentication and security whether the consumer has reasonable access to the data they have provided and/or derived from nonpublic records to verify that the data remain accurate and have not been modified or corrupted.
- Determine whether access to the data has been granted to appropriate parties.
- Determine whether individuals accessing personal data have a need to know and whether this is otherwise consistent with their functional responsibilities.
- Identify processes in place to ensure the authentication and integrity of the individuals accessing the data.
- Understand the levels of access granted to the specific individuals with the degree of access determined by job function.

- Understand whether there are reasonable measures for physically securing data from theft, loss, alteration, or destruction (i.e., physical security of facility).
- Determine whether application, system, and service changes are properly authorized, tested, and promoted into production.

Application Controls

- Identify all collection points, movement, processing, storage, output/reporting to ensure data protection, including transmission over public communication lines, Internet, etc.
- Document the application controls in place to ensure consumer information confidentiality, such as use of leased lines, encryption, etc.
- Document the procedures and controls in place for creating, maintaining, using, or disseminating records of consumer information.
- Evaluate authentication, authorization, integrity, and confidentiality controls implemented programmatically.
- Determine the security controls in place over the Web servers and databases storing consumer information, which prevent unauthorized access to this information.

Security Architecture and Infrastructure Attributes

- Evaluate effectiveness of network/infrastructure authentication controls.
- Evaluate authentication/authorization controls at the operating system level.
- Evaluate Web server configuration settings against corporate policy and effective practices, and ensure appropriate security and configuration patches and fixes have been applied.
- Evaluate the file system configuration (operating systems' security controls over files and databases; access control lists) to verify that individuals have appropriate access to information.
- Evaluate IT operations/general computer controls, including physical protection of data and management of encryption keys where encryption and public key infrastructure processes are used.

Monitoring Controls

- Determine verification process designed to ensure that privacy practices have been implemented as stated in the privacy statement.
- Understand the methods used for allowing consumers to voice their complaints.
- Determine whether there are follow-up procedures to resolve complaints and whether they are operating effectively.

- Determine whether there are other third-party assurances or certifications that validate the effectiveness of privacy controls or otherwise increase customer or individual's confidence and trust in the organization.

Offline Data Collection and Management Processes

- Determine whether data is collected offline, e.g., phone, fax, conferences, etc.
- Determine whether offline data collection practices and uses are consistent with privacy statements and organization policies and practices.

Other Areas to be Addressed

- Data flows
- Agents, third parties, and secondary use of information
- Legal involvement and effectiveness

Detailed Project Program

PROGRAM OBJECTIVE	REF #	PROGRAM ACTIVITY	SUMMARY OF PROGRAM RESULTS
Privacy Statement – General	A1	Identify the business owner(s) for the business unit/application subject to review. *Note: Business owner(s) may be responsible for owning multiple products, and products may be marketed on multiple sites.*	
	A2	Work with the business owner(s) to identify the key business and groups that will be involved in the project.	
	A3	Schedule an introduction meeting with the business owner and key business groups and/or management to ensure that all persons have been advised of the project and clearly understand the project objectives, scope, and reporting process.	
	A4	Determine if a privacy statement (online or other — e.g., verbiage to be included in mailings, phone scripts, etc.) exists that explains the following: • What information is collected. • Who is collecting the information (the organization or an outside third party). • The intended use of the information collected (including whether the information is used for secondary purposes). • The identity of the third parties to whom the organization will disclose the information collected if OK with consumer. • How information collected is stored and secured from unauthorized access. • What choices consumers have over the information collected. • How consumers can access their information collected to update or edit this information. • How consumers can access their information collected to delete this information.	

The Institute of Internal Auditors Research Foundation

PROGRAM OBJECTIVE	REF #	PROGRAM ACTIVITY	SUMMARY OF PROGRAM RESULTS
	A5	Determine if the following terms are defined on the site or in the privacy statement: • Personally identifiable information • Consumer • Third party • Express parental consent *Note: This testing activity is not a requirement for privacy compliance, but is recommended as an effective practice.*	
	A6	Determine if the site has obtained any Privacy Seals (i.e., TRUSTe, BBBOnline, WebTrust, or another outside third-party verification).	
	A7	Confirm the placement of clear and prominent hyperlink or button labeled PRIVACY STATEMENT on home page.	
	A8	Confirm that a PRIVACY STATEMENT hyperlink/button directly links to the privacy statement screen.	
	A9	Confirm that the PRIVACY STATEMENT screen will not disappear unless the consumer closes the screen or navigates to another page on the site.	
	A10	Confirm the existence of a clear and prominent hyperlink statement in bold on the privacy statement page: NOTICE: For important information about safe surfing, see http://www.ftc.gov/bcp/conline/pubs/online/sitesee.html *Note: This testing activity is not a requirement for privacy compliance, but is recommended as an effective practice.*	

The Institute of Internal Auditors Research Foundation

PROGRAM OBJECTIVE	REF #	PROGRAM ACTIVITY	SUMMARY OF PROGRAM RESULTS
Privacy Statement – Control *Environment & Awareness*	**B1**	Identify the individual(s) within the business unit who assume responsibilities for privacy.	
	B2	Determine what procedures/methods the business unit uses to inform the following groups about business unit's privacy policies and practices: • Board of directors, officers, and executive management • Employees and outside contractors • Consumers • Vendors and other third parties	
	B3	Determine whether any documented privacy awareness policies and procedures have been developed and implemented.	
	B4	Determine whether a formal privacy awareness training program has been developed and implemented to communicate privacy procedures and issues to individuals employed or affiliated with the business unit.	
	B5	Obtain content of privacy awareness policies and procedures (or privacy awareness training program, if applicable) and confirm that it contains material about the business unit or site-specific privacy policies, information security procedures, and disciplinary procedures.	
	B6	Obtain content of privacy awareness policies and procedures (or privacy awareness training program, if applicable) and confirm that it contains material about privacy policies. Ensure that all material changes to existing privacy policies are reviewed and approved by legal counsel, and that all third-party contracts include privacy compliance requirements.	

PROGRAM OBJECTIVE	REF #	PROGRAM ACTIVITY	SUMMARY OF PROGRAM RESULTS
	B7	Obtain a list of the following groups: • Board of directors, officers • Executive management • Employees and outside contractors	
	B8	For the listing obtained above, select a sample of 10 individuals and confirm acknowledgment and acceptance of privacy awareness policies and procedures.	
	B9	Document how consumer acknowledgment and acceptance of privacy awareness policies and procedures is obtained prior to the collection of information (i.e., selecting "I Agree" button prior to being provided with an information collection page).	
	B10	Document how third-party and vendor acknowledgment and acceptance of privacy awareness policies and procedures is obtained prior to engaging in the business relationship (i.e., business contract with clause regarding adherence to stated privacy policies and practices).	
Privacy Statement – Content *Information Collection & Intended Use*	C1	Obtain technical documentation detailing site content (i.e., site diagram/application architecture).	
	C2	Identify all pages/methods of collecting information.	
	C3	For each page/information collection method identified, determine what specific types of information the site is collecting. Information includes, but is not limited to: • Personally identifiable information (PII)* (first and last name, zip code, physical address, e-mail address, gender, birth date, and member name).	

The Institute of Internal Auditors Research Foundation

PROGRAM OBJECTIVE	REF #	PROGRAM ACTIVITY	SUMMARY OF PROGRAM RESULTS
		• General (area code, employment information, education level, income, marital status, occupation, interests, and other "demographic" information). • Browser (IP address, operating system, browser software, cookie). • Financial (loan/mortgage information, i.e., purchase/refinance transaction information; borrower information, current housing information, asset and liability information). • Sensitive (credit card numbers, health characteristics and medical information). *Note: The FTC defines PII as information that includes, but is not limited to, first and last name, home or other physical address (e.g., school), e-mail address, telephone number, or any information that identifies a specific individual, or any information which when tied to the above becomes identifiable to a specific individual.*	
	C4	Determine whether the site/application collects any information about consumers from public record, publication, or private organizations.	
	C5	Determine whether the site/application collects any prospect information. *Note: Prospect information is defined as information about one person that is submitted by someone else. For example a name/shipping address for a purchase (i.e., gift) that differs from the purchaser's name/billing address. It can also be the name and phone number/e-mail address on a referral.*	
	C6	For information documented above, determine which information collected is mandatory vs. optional.	

PROGRAM OBJECTIVE	REF #	PROGRAM ACTIVITY	SUMMARY OF PROGRAM RESULTS
	C7	Determine whether the consumer has been notified of the types of information collected and whether this information is mandatory or optional.	
	C8	Document the consequences, if any, of an individual's refusal to provide information or of an individual's decision to opt out of a particular use of such information.	
	C9	Determine whether the consumer is notified of any non-PII information which when tied to PII collected becomes identifiable to that specific individual.	
	C10	Determine whether the consumer is notified of any prospect information collected about them. Document the method by which the consumer is notified (i.e., e-mail, fax, phone, etc.).	
	C11	Select a sample of pages identified above.	
	C12	For sample selected, attempt to submit information online without completing "mandatory" fields. Confirm that submission of information was denied.	
	C13	For sample selected, attempt to submit information online without completing "optional" fields. Confirm that submission of information was accepted.	
	C14	Determine whether a bold, personal collection notice exists on each page that collects personally identifiable information. **Notice: We collect personally identifiable information on this page. Click here to learn more about how we use this information.** *Note: This testing activity is not a requirement for privacy compliance, but is recommended as an effective practice.*	
	C15	Click on the bold, personal collection notice and confirm that the privacy statement screen appears.	

PROGRAM OBJECTIVE	REF #	PROGRAM ACTIVITY	SUMMARY OF PROGRAM RESULTS
	C16	For information collected without a user's explicit knowledge (i.e., browser information), obtain an entry from a log file and confirm that only information documented above is being collected.	
	C17	Determine who is collecting the information (the organization or an outside third party) documented above.	
	C18	Determine whether the consumer has been notified who is collecting the information (the organization or an outside third party).	
	C19	Determine methods used by the site to collect information (i.e., registration forms, feedback forms, contests forms, request forms, order forms, surveys, chat rooms, news groups, forums, mail to forms, bulletin boards) documented above.	
	C20	Determine whether the consumer has been notified of the type and frequency of communications they should expect to receive in the future.	
	C21	Determine the intended use of the information collected above.	
	C22	Based on the intended use of the information, determine that only relevant data is collected — not excessive data in relation to the purpose/ purposes for which they are collected. For example, if a customer is registering a product for personal use — organization name and title should not be collected.	
	C23	Determine the secondary uses of information documented above (e.g., sales and marketing profiling/demographics, third-party fulfillment, selling the information, related third-party product offerings, etc.).	
	C24	Determine whether the consumer has been notified of both the primary and secondary intended use of the information collected above.	

PROGRAM OBJECTIVE	REF #	PROGRAM ACTIVITY	SUMMARY OF PROGRAM RESULTS
	C25	Identify all pages that are sponsoring an activity.	
	C26	For each page identified above, determine if the consumer has been notified who is sponsoring the activity (the organization or an outside third party).	
	C27	Determine whether individuals are given the opportunity to opt out of secondary use of their data (by either the organization or an outside party). Is the opt-out/opt-in method utilized and is it active or passive (i.e., is the box pre-checked or not checked?).	
	C28	If the Web site uses cookies, how are they used and what are the consequences, if any, of an individual's refusal to accept a cookie?	
Privacy Statement – Content *Sharing Information*	D1	Identify the third parties (i.e., vendors, business partners, outside agents, etc.) to whom the organization will disclose the information collected if consumer consents.	
	D2	Document the method by which consent is given.	
	D3	Determine whether the consumer has been notified of the third parties (i.e., vendors, business partners, outside agents, etc.) to whom the organization will disclose the information collected if consumer consents.	
	D4	Determine how these third parties intend to use the consumer's information.	
	D5	Determine the secondary uses of information shared with third parties (e.g., sales and marketing profiling/demographics, third-party fulfillment, selling the information, related third-party product offerings, etc.).	
	D6	Determine whether the consumer has been notified of both the primary and secondary intended use of the information shared with third parties.	

The Institute of Internal Auditors Research Foundation

PROGRAM OBJECTIVE	REF #	PROGRAM ACTIVITY	SUMMARY OF PROGRAM RESULTS
	D7	Determine the methods the organization will use to share or transfer information collected from a consumer to a third party (i.e., ftp, fax, e-mail, mail, etc.).	
	D8	Determine whether the consumer has been notified regarding the methods the organization will use to share or transfer information collected from a consumer to a third party.	
	D9	Determine whether the consumer has been notified of the type and frequency of communications they should expect to receive from these third parties in the future.	
	D10	If the site refers or links consumers to a third party's site, determine whether the consumer is notified they are leaving the organization site.	
	D11	Determine whether the organization has business agreements or contracts with third parties to whom the organization shares consumer information.	
	D12	Determine whether the organization has business agreements or contracts with third parties to whom the organization refers or links consumers.	
	D13	Obtain a sample of business agreements or contracts and confirm that (1) the third party is required to adhere to the organization's stated Privacy Policies and (2) the organization is indemnified against any misuse of consumer information by the third party.	
	D14	Document procedures in place to discontinue or terminate business relationships with third parties that fail to adhere to the organization's stated privacy policies.	

PROGRAM OBJECTIVE	REF #	PROGRAM ACTIVITY	SUMMARY OF PROGRAM RESULTS
	D15	Determine whether the organization requires third parties with whom information is shared or to whose sites consumers are referred or linked to have detailed privacy policies. *Note: Consider using the organization's privacy policy as a benchmark or Privacy Seal programs (i.e., BBBOnline or TRUSTe) eligibility criteria for appropriate privacy statement content.*	
	D16	Examine the privacy policies (online or other) for a sample of third-party business partners and confirm that the privacy policies are consistent with content set forth in the organization's privacy policy or Privacy Seal program eligibility criteria.	
	D17	Consider selecting a sample of business partners or third parties affiliated with the site and requesting that independent verification be obtained, either by the organization's internal audit or another third party, regarding compliance with stated privacy policies.	
	D18	Document procedures in place to discontinue or terminate business relationships with third parties who fail to post detailed privacy policies on their site or are in noncompliance with their stated privacy policies.	
	D19	Determine whether the organization shares or transfers consumer information with its subsidiaries. Determine what business rules exist and are being applied to restrict access of data to particular subsidiary locations/countries.	
	D20	For consumer information shared or transferred to international subsidiaries, document procedures to ensure compliance with privacy laws and regulations of that applicable country.	
	D21	Determine whether the consumer has been notified which subsidiaries their consumer information was shared.	

The Institute of Internal Auditors Research Foundation

PROGRAM OBJECTIVE	REF #	PROGRAM ACTIVITY	SUMMARY OF PROGRAM RESULTS
Privacy Statement – Content *Information Storage*	E1	Obtain diagram of network topography supporting site.	
	E2	Identify the main characteristics of systems and environments, specifically: • Key systems. • In-house or packaged software applications. • Computer processing locations. • Hardware environments (i.e., servers/ databases). • Internal and external network connections. • Use of new or emerging technologies (i.e., SSL, cryptography, PGP, etc.).	
	E3	Determine whether the site uses a standard or secure server.	
	E4	Determine the existence of a firewall.	
	E5	Determine the storage location (i.e., file directory, database, etc.) for consumer information collected.	
	E6	Obtain database table schema and identify tables populated with information collected.	
	E7	Confirm, via query statement, that information submitted in Information Collection and Use (above) is properly stored in the database.	
	E8	Select a sample of servers hosting the site and confirm the following: • Log file paths are correctly configured. • General and advanced logging options are enabled to record visitor information daily.	
	E9	Determine that a data retention policy exists and contains a purging schedule appropriate for the type of data collected and its use.	

PROGRAM OBJECTIVE	REF #	PROGRAM ACTIVITY	SUMMARY OF PROGRAM RESULTS
	E10	Determine whether the consumer is notified about the organization's storage processes and locations, as well as the length of time their information is maintained in the organization's systems.	
	E11	Determine if any business processes subvert security practices. For example, ensure that any information provided by the customer securely (e.g., SSL) is kept secure and not returned to them in plaintext e-mail from a CSR or other means.	
	E12	Confirm, via query statement, that information edited/updated in Information Choices (above) is properly reflected in the database.	
	E13	Confirm, via query statement, that information deleted in Information Choices (above), is properly reflected in the database.	
	E14	Determine third parties' storage locations (i.e., file directory, database, etc.) for consumer information shared with the third party by the organization.	
	E15	Determine whether the consumer is notified about the third parties' storage processes and locations, as well as the length of time their information is maintained in the third parties' systems.	
Privacy Statement – Content *Information Choices*	F1	Determine whether the consumer is given the choice to use a standard or secure server to submit information.	
	F2	Determine if the consumer is notified about the benefits of using a secure server.	
	F3	Determine if the consumer is notified of the risks involved with using a standard server.	

PROGRAM OBJECTIVE	REF #	PROGRAM ACTIVITY	SUMMARY OF PROGRAM RESULTS
	F4	Determine if a notice exists on the site that explains how consumers can access their information stored in the organization or a third party's systems (i.e., opt-out box, via e-mail, "reply" to unsubscribe, via telephone, etc.).	
	F5	For information stored in the organization's systems, determine whether the consumer has the ability to personally access their information to update or change information.	
	F6	Document authentication mechanisms (i.e., user login id/password) in place to validate that only the consumer and not an unauthorized party can access the consumer's information stored in the organization systems.	
	F7	Attempt to access another consumer's information and confirm that access was denied.	
	F8	Acting as a consumer, attempt to access information submitted in Information Collection and Use: Activity 10 and confirm the existence of an authentication mechanism (i.e., user login id/password).	
	F9	Provide invalid password and confirm that attempt to access information was denied.	
	F10	Make edits or updates to information and confirm that changes were accepted.	
	F11	If consumers do not have the option to access their information themselves, document how consumers can make a request to the organization to update or edit their information.	
	F12	Document authentication mechanisms in place to validate that only the consumer and not an unauthorized party can make a request to have their information updated or edited.	
	F13	Acting as a consumer, make a request to have your information updated or edited and confirm the existence of an authentication mechanism (i.e., user login id/password).	

The Institute of Internal Auditors Research Foundation

PROGRAM OBJECTIVE	REF #	PROGRAM ACTIVITY	SUMMARY OF PROGRAM RESULTS
	F14	Confirm that updates or edits were processed in a timely manner.	
	F15	For information shared with third parties, determine whether the third party provides the consumer with a means to edit/update or make a request to edit/update information stored in third parties' systems.	
	F16	Determine if a notice exists on the site that explains how consumers can delete their information stored in the organization or a third parties' systems (i.e., opt-out box, via e-mail, "reply" to unsubscribe, via telephone, etc.).	
	F17	For information stored in the organization's systems, determine whether the consumer has the ability to personally access the information to delete the information.	
	F18	Document authentication mechanisms (i.e., user login id/password) in place to validate that only the consumer and not an unauthorized party can delete the consumer's information stored in the organization systems.	
	F19	Acting as a consumer, attempt to delete information submitted in Information Collection and Use (above) and confirm the existence of an authentication mechanism (i.e. user login id/password).	
	F20	Either delete information or select the "opt-out" box and confirm that request was accepted.	
	F21	If consumers do not have the option to access their information themselves, document how they can make a request to the organization to delete their information.	
	F22	For information shared with third parties, determine whether the third party provides the consumer with a means to delete or make a request to delete information stored in that third party's systems.	

PROGRAM OBJECTIVE	REF #	PROGRAM ACTIVITY	SUMMARY OF PROGRAM RESULTS
	F23	For financial and sensitive information documented in Information Collected (above), determine whether a specific "opt-in" box exists on the pages where this information is collected.	
	F24	For prospect information documented in Information Collected (above), determine what choices the individual, about whom the information was collected, has over the use of this information or the sharing of this information with third parties. For example, must the organization obtain written consent from the individual in order to: • Collect the information? • Share the information with a third party? • Store the information in the organization's systems?	
Privacy Statement – Security General Computer Controls *System Maintenance*	G1	Document the site's system maintenance activities and controls, including: • Specification, tracking, and authorization of change requests. • Unit, system, and user testing. • Authorization of transfers to the live environment. • Updating user technical documentation and training. • Database administration.	
	G2	Determine if application development and change control policies and procedures exist for back-end changes (i.e., Web/database scripts and applications).	
	G3	Determine whether back-end change requests are formally made (i.e., via Change or New Project Request forms), logged, and reviewed and approved by the appropriate management.	
	G4	Determine whether developers test back-end changes before being migrated into production.	

PROGRAM OBJECTIVE	REF #	PROGRAM ACTIVITY	SUMMARY OF PROGRAM RESULTS
	G5	Determine whether QA staff tests back-end changes before being migrated into production.	
	G6	Confirm that developers responsible for making back-end changes cannot migrate these changes into production.	
	G7	Determine whether change management or control versioning software (i.e., VSS) is used to log back-end changes and whether these logs are monitored for changes.	
	G8	Determine if site editing policies and procedures exist for front-end changes (i.e., HTML content).	
	G9	Obtain site editing policies and procedures and confirm that certain types of pages must be reviewed and approved by the person responsible for privacy (i.e., compliance officer) prior to being promoted onto the live site. For example: • All new form pages with fields for collection of consumer information. • All current pages collecting personally identifiable information (PII). • All edits to the privacy statement pages. • All edits to pages that require a consumer to provide the organization with authorization prior to sharing information collected with a third party.	
	G10	Determine whether front-end change requests are formally made (i.e., via Change or New Project Request forms), logged, and reviewed and approved by the appropriate management.	
	G11	Determine whether all site content changes are tested by Web masters and reviewed by QA.	
	G12	Confirm that developers responsible for making front-end changes cannot migrate these changes into production.	

PROGRAM OBJECTIVE	REF #	PROGRAM ACTIVITY	SUMMARY OF PROGRAM RESULTS
	G13	Determine whether change management or control versioning software (i.e., VSS) is used to log front-end changes and whether these logs are monitored for changes.	
	G14	Determine whether monitoring procedures are in place that provide reasonable assurance of the following: • Business practice disclosures on the Web site remain current. • Reports of noncompliance are promptly addressed and corrective measures are taken.	

Privacy Statement – Security General Computer Controls *Information Security*	H1	Obtain the site's or organization's security policy and confirm that written policies cover(s):
		a) General
		  • Legal and regulatory compliance concerning the protection of information.
		  • Integrity, confidentiality, and availability.
		  • Employee responsibility.
		b) Campus Access Procedures
		  • Description of procedures for identification badges, card readers, physical locks, etc.
		  • Access procedures for visitors, contractors, and temporary help.
		  • Description of security resources.
		  • Responsibility of managers, employees, security guards, etc.
		c) Online Security Procedures
		  • Unique IDs
		  • Access levels.
		  • Passwords.
		  • Frequency of password changes.
		  • User access controls.
		  • Filtering mechanisms.
		d) Internet Security Procedures
		e) Employees
		  • Employee monitoring procedures.
		  • Remedial action for illicit activity.	

PROGRAM OBJECTIVE	REF #	PROGRAM ACTIVITY	SUMMARY OF PROGRAM RESULTS
	H2	Determine how the organization communicates security policies and procedures to employees, outside contractors, third parties, etc. (i.e., user security education and training program).	
	H3	Determine how many system administrators (SAs) and database administrators (DBAs) are responsible for controlling and managing information collected and stored in the business unit's systems.	
	H4	Identify roles and responsibilities for SAs and DBAs.	
	H5	Determine all other individuals within the business unit and/or organization that have access to consumer information and the level of access granted.	
	H6	Determine if controls are in place to protect transmission of private customer information over the Internet from unintended recipients (e.g., encryption technology, SSL, certificates, etc.).	
	H7	Determine whether the organization requires all employees to sign Nondisclosure Agreements (NDAs) prior to accessing consumer information stored in the organization's systems.	
	H8	Determine if access to consumer information is granted to parties outside the business unit and/or organization. If so, determine whether there are controls in place to: • Ensure appropriate use of consumer information by third parties. • Limit unauthorized access and use of this information.	
	H9	Determine whether the organization requires third parties and outside contractors to sign NDAs prior to accessing consumer information stored in the organization's systems.	

PROGRAM OBJECTIVE	REF #	PROGRAM ACTIVITY	SUMMARY OF PROGRAM RESULTS
	H10	Determine whether the organization requires third parties to sign agreements to obtain access to data. Determine the process in place to notify the security administrator when the agreement is terminated or modified.	
	H11	Document and evaluate the process for authorizing and creating user access to consumer information. Also, do any documented policies exist for creating and approving new user accounts or modifying existing user account profiles? Confirm whether an audit trail is maintained for new user access requests.	
	H12	Document termination and department transfer procedures to ensure that access to consumer information is revoked in a timely manner.	
	H13	Document procedures for performing periodic review of user access to ensure that privileges are commensurate with a user's job responsibilities.	
	H14	Determine the physical location of the computer facilities.	
	H15	Document physical security controls over the computer facilities and the building where the computer facilities are located.	
	H16	Determine how users are granted access to the computer facilities.	
	H17	Document termination and department transfer procedures to ensure that access to computer facilities is revoked in a timely manner.	
	H18	Document procedures for performing periodic review of user access to ensure that privileges are commensurate with a user's job responsibilities.	

PROGRAM OBJECTIVE	REF #	PROGRAM ACTIVITY	SUMMARY OF PROGRAM RESULTS
	H19	Determine if the organization monitors access to the computer facilities. For example, security cameras, mantraps, cardkey access, visitor's log and badges.	
	H20	Determine whether the computer facilities have proper environmental controls (i.e., air conditioners, smoke detectors, humidifiers, sprinklers, etc.).	
	H21	Determine whether the computer facilities have backup power (i.e., battery, UPS, generators, etc.).	
	H22	Controls are maintained so that individually identifiable information collected, created, or maintained is accurate and complete for its intended use.	
	H23	Controls are maintained to protect against unauthorized access to customer's computers and unauthorized modification of customer's computer files.	
	H24	Customer permission is obtained before storing, altering, or copying information in the customer's computer, or the customer is notified with an option to prevent such activities.	
	H25	Programming standards have been implemented and software testing is conducted to ensure Web pages using active content technologies (e.g., Java applets, ActiveX, JavaScript) are not susceptible to security weaknesses.	
	H26	Monitoring procedures are in place to provide reasonable assurance that: • Information protection controls remain effective. • Reports of noncompliance are promptly addressed. • Corrective measures are taken.	

PROGRAM OBJECTIVE	REF #	PROGRAM ACTIVITY	SUMMARY OF PROGRAM RESULTS
Privacy Statement – Security General Computer Controls *Computer Operations*	I1	Document procedures to recover computer systems in the event of a natural disaster or extended recovery delay (i.e., Business Continuity Plan or Disaster Recovery Plan).	
	I2	Determine whether roles and responsibilities for computer operations staff are clearly defined.	
	I3	Determine whether batch processing occurs and the frequency.	
	I4	Determine which individuals with the organization or business unit can create, modify, or delete a batch job.	
	I5	Determine how computer operations staff is notified of failed/successful batch jobs.	
	I6	Document information archiving and tape backup procedures, including: • Which systems (i.e., databases and servers) are backed up. • Information (incremental vs. full) that is backed up and the frequency (daily vs. weekly). • How often tapes are rotated off-site. • Tape-recycling procedures. • Individuals responsible for tape backups and transfer to off-site storage.	
	I7	Obtain documented tape backup and off-site transfer procedures.	
	I8	Document procedures to test restoration and recovery from an operational failure.	
	I9	Document procedures for upgrading existing or implementing new system software.	
	I10	Determine if virus checks are performed on all PCs and servers.	

PROGRAM OBJECTIVE	REF #	PROGRAM ACTIVITY	SUMMARY OF PROGRAM RESULTS
	I11	Procedures should be formalized to ensure that development and maintenance groups keep current on the latest security bugs and hacker exploits. For example, the Computer Emergency Response Team (CERT) maintains an e-mail distribution list communicating current security vulnerabilities within operating systems and application platforms. Popular "bugtraq" mailing lists are also an effective way to identify security exploits.	
Privacy Statement – Security Application Controls *External Users (Consumers)*	J1	Document the authentication procedures to verify the identity of the consumer accessing the data (i.e., unique user id and password; group id and shared password). *Refer to Information Choices (above) for further details of testing executed.*	
	J2	Document whether multiple users can access the same consumer information.	
	J3	Document the number of failed login attempts that will result in a user being locked out of the system.	
	J4	Document how the user obtains a "forgotten" password or requests that their password be reset in the event they are logged off after "x" failed login attempts.	
	J5	Document whether the application automatically logs the user off of the system after a period of inactivity. Also, document the length of time a user's terminal must be inactive prior to being logged off.	

The Institute of Internal Auditors Research Foundation

PROGRAM OBJECTIVE	REF #	PROGRAM ACTIVITY	SUMMARY OF PROGRAM RESULTS
	J6	Document the authentication procedures to verify the identity of the internal user accessing the data (i.e., unique user id and password; group id and shared password). *Note: Consider both internal and external access points (i.e., Internet, local terminals, databases, servers, remote dialup, etc.).*	
	J7	Document whether internal users (i.e., employees) are limited to accessing consumer information from dedicated terminals or machines.	
	J8	Document whether multiple internal users can access the same consumer information.	
	J9	Document and evaluate password parameters: • Minimum password length (six to eight characters). • Alphanumeric password combination. • Maximum password age allowed (i.e., 30 days). • Password history (i.e., can't use previous 10 passwords). • Content guidelines of passwords in place (i.e., easily guessable password, must differ from user's login name, must differ by at least three characters from previous password).	
	J10	Document the number of failed login attempts that will result in an internal user being locked out of the system. *Note: Consider the following systems (i.e., work terminal, server, database, etc.).*	
	J11	Document how the internal user obtains a "forgotten" password or requests that their password be reset in the event they are logged off after "x" failed login attempts. For example, is account locked for one hour or until an administrator re-enables the account? *Note: Ensure that password reset requests are formal and not granted on voice recognition.*	

The Institute of Internal Auditors Research Foundation

PROGRAM OBJECTIVE	REF #	PROGRAM ACTIVITY	SUMMARY OF PROGRAM RESULTS
	J12	Document whether the option to automatically log the internal user off of the system (Internet, local terminals, databases, servers, remote dialup) after a period of inactivity is enabled.	
	J13	Document additional authentication requirements (i.e., Xircom card, dual authentication) for remote dial-in access.	
	J14	Determine what operating and database management system security is in place to ensure that consumer information, maintained in the organization's systems (i.e., local hard drive, servers, and databases), is secure from unauthorized access.	
	J15	Obtain an access control listing of all internal users with access to consumer information collected on the site. Identify the system to which they have access and the level of access granted to each internal user (i.e., read, write, change, full control, etc.).	
	J16	Select samples from the listing obtained above and confirm that the system to which they have access and the level of access granted is commensurate with job responsibilities.	
	J17	Determine whether sensitive information (e.g., credit card numbers, social security numbers, health and medical history) is stored separately from other information collected.	
	J18	Determine if sensitive data is stored in encrypted database tables.	
	J19	Determine if additional authentication procedures are necessary to access sensitive or encrypted data.	
	J20	Determine how the organization monitors access to sensitive information and whether sensitive information is restricted to a limited number of users.	

PROGRAM OBJECTIVE	REF #	PROGRAM ACTIVITY	SUMMARY OF PROGRAM RESULTS
	J21	Determine the procedures in place for merging files/databases, specifically as it relates to maintaining the integrity of customer preferences on use of data (i.e., opt-in/opt-out elections, etc.).	
Privacy Statement – Security Monitoring Controls	K1	Document how computer monitors network activity (i.e., server load balance, database utilization). For example, does the system rely on daemons or other commercial utilities to monitor the network?	
	K2	Document how management is notified of network activity (i.e., e-mail, online reports, hardcopy reports).	
	K3	Determine who reviews these network activity reports and how often.	
	K4	Determine how the organization monitors access to sensitive systems and databases.	
	K5	Determine whether there is a security audit log to record information such as the date/time of each event, user identity, and success/failure of the event. Also, determine whether the system/ application associates any auditable events with the actual identity (i.e., name/computer terminal) of the user who caused the events.	
	K6	Determine whether the ability to create, delete, or modify the security audit log is limited to authorized IT personnel.	
	K7	Determine who reviews the security audit logs (specifically access violation reports) and how often.	
	K8	Document procedures in place to address an external or internal breach of security. For example, attempted or successful breaches to the computing environment or unauthorized access to consumer information.	

The Institute of Internal Auditors Research Foundation

PROGRAM OBJECTIVE	REF #	PROGRAM ACTIVITY	SUMMARY OF PROGRAM RESULTS
	K9	Identify the storage location for sensitive printouts and security audit logs and document processes for destroying this information.	
	K10	Determine how legal counsel is informed of privacy statement changes or site content changes that affect statements disclosed in the site's/business unit's privacy statement.	
	K11	Document the process for obtaining review and approval from legal counsel for all privacy-related changes, including detailed privacy practices.	
	K12	Document procedures used by the individual responsible for privacy (i.e., compliance officer) to ensure that the site is maintaining compliance with stated privacy policies.	
	K13	Determine whether the individual responsible for privacy (i.e., compliance officer) performs periodic compliance audits over the site to confirm that the language does not need to be added/modified/deleted from the privacy statement.	
	K14	For audits performed above, obtain reports and review results and recommendations to determine if further privacy work by internal audit is deemed necessary.	
	K15	Determine if the consumer has been notified how to contact the site or organization if they have a complaint or suggestion about the privacy statement or any content on the site.	
	K16	Determine if the consumer has been notified how to contact the site or organization if they have a complaint about a third party with whom the site or organization shares information, refers or links to, or has any type of business relationship.	
	K17	Document the process by which a consumer can submit a complaint or suggestion.	

The Institute of Internal Auditors Research Foundation

PROGRAM OBJECTIVE	REF #	PROGRAM ACTIVITY	SUMMARY OF PROGRAM RESULTS
	K18	Document how complaints and suggestions are processed and addressed by the site or organization. For example, does the business maintain a log of all consumer complaints and suggestions?	
	K19	Determine whether the consumer is notified of when they can expect to receive a response to their complaint or suggestion. For example, language stating "we will process and reply to your suggestion within three business days."	
	K20	Submit a suggestion or complaint and specify that a return response is desired. Confirm whether a response was received in a timely manner and within the time frame described on the site.	
	K21	Document the method by which the site or organization responds to the consumer's complaint or suggestion.	
	K22	Document the process for following up on and addressing consumer complaints and suggestions.	
	K23	Determine what happens to the consumer's information once the complaint or suggestion has been addressed (i.e., e-mail address, phone number, etc.).	
	K24	Determine how long consumer complaints and suggestions are maintained.	
	K25	Select samples of consumer complaints and/or suggestions received in a specific time frame (i.e., the prior 12 months) and confirm that all communications were appropriately addressed and no significant or unusual issues or problems were unresolved.	

The Institute of Internal Auditors Research Foundation

APPENDIX A
SAMPLE WEB SITE
PRIVACY STATEMENT

This document was last updated {specify date}.

{Organization} is committed to protecting your privacy. You can visit most pages on our site without giving us any information about yourself. But sometimes we do need information to provide services that you request, and this privacy statement explains data collection and use in those situations. This privacy statement only applies to {Organization}; it does not apply to other online or offline sites, products, or services. Please read the complete {Organization} privacy statement.

Collection of your Personal Information

We will ask you when we need information that personally identifies you (personal information) or allows us to contact you. Generally, this information is requested when you are registering before entering a contest, ordering e-mail newsletters, joining a limited-access premium site, signing up for an event or training, or when purchasing and/or registering {Organization} products. Personal information collected by {Organization} often is limited to e-mail address, language, country, or location, but may include other information when needed to provide a service you requested.

For example: If you choose a service or transaction that requires payment, such as making a purchase, we will request personal information necessary for billing and/or shipping, such as: name, address, telephone number, and credit card number.

When you buy a new product, we may ask you to register your purchase electronically. We keep this registration information on file with any information you've already given us on previous visits to our Web site.

{Organization} also collects certain information about your computer hardware and software. This information may include: your IP address, browser type, operating system, domain name, access times, and referring Web site addresses. This information is used for the operation of the service, to maintain quality of the service, and to provide general statistics regarding use of {Organization}.

The Institute of Internal Auditors Research Foundation

{Organization} also collects information about which pages our customers visit. This site visitation data is identified only by a unique ID number, and it is never linked with personal information unless a user consents as described below.

Use of your Personal Information

We use your personal information for the following purposes:

- To ensure our site is relevant to your needs.
- To deliver services, such as newsletters, events, training, or software that you request or purchase.
- To help us create and publish content most relevant to you.
- To alert you to new products, special offers, updated information, and other new services from {Organization}, if you so request.
- To allow you access to limited-entry areas of our site as appropriate.

We will merge site-visitation data with anonymous demographic information for research purposes, and we may use this information in aggregate to provide more relevant content. In some limited-entry sections of {Organization}, with your approval, we will combine site-visitation data with your personal information in order to provide you with personalized content. If you decline permission, we will not provide you the personalized service and won't merge your personal information with site-visitation data.

We occasionally hire other companies to provide limited services on our behalf, including packaging, mailing, and delivering purchases, answering customer questions about products or services, sending postal mail, and processing event registration. We will only provide those companies the information they need to deliver the service, and they are prohibited from using that information for any other purpose.

{Organization} may disclose your personal information if required to do so by law or in the good-faith belief that such action is necessary to: (a) conform to the edicts of the law or comply with legal process served on {Organization} or the site; (b) protect and defend the rights or property of {Organization} and its Web sites; or (c) act in urgent circumstances to protect the personal safety of {Organization} employees, users of {Organization} products or services, or members of the public.

Your information may be stored and processed in the United States or any other country in which {Organization} or its affiliates, subsidiaries, or agents maintain facilities, and by using this site, you consent to any such transfer of information outside your country. {Organization} abides by the safe harbor framework as set forth by the U.S. Department of Commerce regarding the collection, use, and retention of data from the European Union.

Control of your Personal Information

When you register, or otherwise give us personal information, {Organization} will not share that information with third parties without your permission, other than for the limited exceptions already listed. It will only be used for the purposes stated above.

Access to your Personal Information

We will provide you with the means to ensure that your personal information is correct and current.

If you register on {Organization} Web site or subscribe to a newsletter, you can review and edit your personal information, such as:

- View and edit personal information you have already given us at {Organization}.
- Tell us whether you want {Organization} to send you marketing information.
- Choose whether you want third parties to send you their offers by postal mail.
- Subscribe or cancel subscriptions to newsletters about our services and products.

If you are unable to access your personal information online, you can do so by contacting {Organization} as described at the bottom of this statement.

Security of your Personal Information

{Organization} is committed to protecting the security of your personal information. We use a variety of security technologies and procedures to help protect your personal information from unauthorized access, use, or disclosure. For example, we store the personal information you provide in computer servers with limited access that are located in controlled facilities. When we transmit sensitive information (such as a credit card number) over the Internet, we protect it through the use of encryption, such as the Secure Socket Layer (SSL) protocol.

Protection of Children's Personal Information

{Organization} is a general audience site and does not knowingly collect any personal information from children.

Use of Cookies

When someone visits the site, a cookie is placed on the customer's machine (if the customer accepts cookies) or is read if the customer has visited the site previously. One use of cookies is to assist in the collection of the site visitation statistics described above.

We also use cookies to collect information on which newsletter links are clicked by customers. This information is used to ensure we are sending information customers want to read. It is collected in aggregate form and never linked with your personal information.

Web beacons, also known as clear gif technology, or action tags, may be used to assist in delivering the cookie on our site. This technology tells us how many visitors clicked on key elements (such as links or graphics) on a {Organization} Web page. We do not use this technology to access your personally identifiable information on {Organization}; it is a tool we use to compile aggregated statistics about {Organization} Web site usage. We may share aggregated site statistics with partner companies but do not allow other companies to place clear gifs on our sites.

If you choose to not have your browser accept cookies from the {Organization} Web site, you will be able to view the text on the screens, however you will not experience a personalized visit nor will you be able to subscribe to the service offerings on the site.

Web Site Certification

{Organization} is a member of the {specify program, if applicable}. Because {Organization} wants to demonstrate its commitment to your privacy, we have agreed to publish our information practices and have our privacy practices reviewed for compliance by {specify program}.

Enforcement of this Privacy Statement

If you have questions regarding this statement, you should contact {Organization}.

Changes to this Statement

{Organization} will occasionally update this privacy statement. When we do, we will also revise the "last updated" date at the top of the privacy statement. For material changes to this statement, {Organization} will notify you by placing prominent notice on the Web site.

Contact Information

{Organization} welcomes your comments regarding this privacy statement. Please contact us by e-mail or postal mail.

Organization
Contact Information

Last Updated: {specify date}

APPENDIX B
PRIVACY ENABLERS

Introduction

There are a wide variety of enabling technologies that allow privacy to be protected. Along with developing and promoting privacy policy effectively, one of the challenges today is developing an appropriate response for an organization from all those that are available. The following list has been compiled to identify highly visible vendors and products in the privacy space. It is neither inclusive nor an endorsement of any, but is presented to give an idea of what is out there. The related Web site is listed at the beginning of each section.

A more comprehensive listing of privacy-related Web sites is available from the Electronic Privacy Information Center. See: http://www.epic.org/privacy/privacy_resources_faq.html.

Privacy Enabling Technologies

American Express Private Payments
http://www.americanexpress.com/privatepayments/
American Express Private Payments is a secured way to purchase and pay online without transmitting an actual card account number over the Internet, thus keeping account information private and secure. Use of Private Payments generates a randomly created unique number. The card member transfers this information into the merchant order form to complete the purchase. Members access the service by going to the Private Payments home page at www.americanexpress.com or by clicking on a Private Payments icon on their desktop, if they signed up previously.

The service prompts them to select the American Express® Card they want linked to Private Payments and select a username and password to be used in the future. Private Payments is available to American Express consumer and small business card members in the U.S. The item purchased is charged to the selected card and appears on the monthly billing statement as usual. Since the Private Payments number is used for a single purchase, and expires after the merchant's authorization process is completed, it cannot be used again, so stealing or copying it is pointless.

AT&T
http://www.att.com
This P3P (Platform for Privacy Preferences) user agent is implemented as a browser helper object for Internet Explorer. The software is called AT&T Privacy Bird and it is available at www.privacybird.com. When users install this software, it adds a privacy button to the top of their

browser window. Clicking on this button brings up a window where users can set their privacy preferences, check how well a site's P3P policy matches their preferences, or view a site's privacy policy in P3P or human-readable format. This tool was developed jointly with Microsoft. Additional information about P3P can be found at: http://www.w3.org/P3P/

Microsoft
http://www.microsoft.com
Microsoft's Enhanced Cookie Controls for Internet Explorer (IE) 6.0 allow users to delete all cookies with a single click; give users better information about cookies; and, significantly, will prompt users, by default, when a third party (a site other than the site being visited) attempts to set or read a cookie on the user's hard drive.

Microsoft also offers a Privacy Statement Wizard for small and medium-sized businesses to give them an easy way to develop a privacy policy. The Wizard steps the user through a series of questions about company information practices. On completion, it generates a draft policy. The user can mark the policy with XML tags, a key step toward making the policy P3P compliant.

Microsoft's Kids Passport gives Web sites the means to seek consent from parents to transact online with a child. The requesting Web site must be COPPA-compliant. It gives parents whose children visit those sites the ability to manage the PII given out in compliance with the law.

Netscape
http://www.netscape.com
Netscape Cookie Manager — a feature of the Netscape browser that allows users to view, block, and delete cookies based on their individual privacy preferences. For instance, it allows a user to determine who may and who may not set cookies on the computer, edit and/or delete any of the cookies on the computer, and review a list and detailed description of all the cookies.

P3P
http://www.w3.org/p3p
The Platform for Privacy Preferences Project (P3P), developed by the World Wide Web Consortium, allows users more control over use of personal information on Web sites they visit. Basically, P3P is a standardized set of multiple-choice questions, covering all major aspects of a site's privacy policies, to present a clear snapshot of how a site handles personal information. P3P-enabled Web sites make this information available in a standard, machine-readable format. P3P-enabled browsers can "read" this snapshot and compare it to the consumer's own set of privacy preferences, enhancing user control by putting privacy policies where users can find them, in a form they can understand. Most important, it enables users to act on what they see. When users enter a site equipped with P3P that does not match their privacy preferences, a warning is issued. There is no block; the users can still visit the site if they choose.

Verification and Assurance Programs and Self-Regulatory Efforts

AICPA/CICA WebTrustSM/TM Program
http://www.aicpa.org/assurance/webtrust/princip.htm

- The American Institute of Certified Public Accountants (AICPA) teamed with the Canadian Institute of Chartered Accountants (CICA) to launch WebTrust [SM], an electronic commerce seal designed to help make the Internet a safer place to shop. The seal provides assurances that a Web site meets an established set of principles and criteria (i.e., a standard). One of the principles is online privacy. Binding, third-party arbitration to resolve privacy disputes is also a requirement of the service.

- The WebTrust [SM] Program for Online Privacy allows practitioners to independently verify that the entity's Web site informs customers as to the privacy policies and that the site actually follows those policies. The WebTrust [SM] Online Privacy seal is intended to be a visual representation that a Web site complies with the fair information practices described in the Online Privacy principle. The seal differs from seal programs such as TRUSTe and BBBOnLine in that a Web site must earn the right to display the seal by engaging an independent CPA or CA to perform significant testing of privacy practices before displaying the seal.

- The AICPA Privacy Task Force was formed in late 2001 and has developed a Privacy Framework and a set of awareness and educational tools. The version 1.0 releases are due out by mid-2003. The privacy principles in the Privacy Framework are not oriented to only online privacy. They were developed through analysis of the common requirements of a number of worldwide privacy laws and regulations. The Privacy Framework will replace the Online Privacy principle currently used in the WebTrust [SM] and SysTrust [SM] products.

BBBOnLine
http://www.bbbonline.org/privacy

- BBBOnLine operates two self-regulatory, online privacy seal programs: (1) Privacy, and (2) Kid's Privacy. An excellent Privacy Assessment Questionnaire is available on the site as is the privacy standard itself in the OnLine Reliability Program and Kid's Privacy Program information. BBBOnLine is the second most numerous privacy seal for providing assurance in the B2C marketplace. BBBOnLine seals cost from $200 to $7,000 annually (data as of February 2003).

Individual Reference Services Group (IRSG)
http://www.irsg.org
- This is a group of information companies that developed a set of self-regulatory principles to govern the dissemination and use of personal data through individual reference services. Companies that sign on to the IRSG principles commit, among other things, to:
  - Acquire individually identifiable information only from sources known as reputable,
  - Restrict their distribution of non-public information through safeguards appropriately calibrated to the type of use made of the information,
  - Educate the public about their database services, and
  - Furnish individuals with information contained in services and products that specifically identifies them, unless the information is publicly available or a matter of public record, in which case the companies will provide the individuals with guidance on how they can obtain the information from the original source.

- The Federal Trade Commission approved the principles.

Network Advertising Initiative (NAI)
http://www.networkadvertising.org
- In November 1999, the FTC held a series of workshops focusing on online profiling by Web advertisers. Under examination was the use of "cookies" to covertly track Web usage, as well as the potential for linking anonymous Web-based profiles with real-world information, including names and addresses. The most publicized example of this was the announced merger of online advertiser DoubleClick with offline marketing company Abacus Direct. Concerned, the FTC suggested that the network advertising industry launch a mechanism for policing itself or the FTC would fill the void.

- The eight largest industry players formed a group called the Network Advertising Initiative (NAI) and drafted a set of principles that they then shared with the FTC. On July 27, 2000, the FTC voted 4-1 to endorse the self-regulatory plan. Privacy advocates objected, calling it "written by industry for industry" and saying it fails to adequately address the issue. The NAI principles require the "opt-out" form of consent as opposed to "opt-in."

- One of the principles the group relies on is periodic verification by independent service providers that NAI companies are complying with their posted privacy policies. The NAI and its Members have engaged TRUSTe to create and manage an independent program for the purpose of ensuring that the NAI Members comply with the NAI Self-Regulatory Principles. As the manager of this program, TRUSTe is using a publicly available Web site (http://www.truste.org/users/users_watchdog_intro.html) for registering complaints from Web users alleging noncompliance with the NAI Principles. TRUSTe's role in this program is to receive and investigate complaints, independent of the NAI and its Members. TRUSTe, independent of the NAI and its Members, manages the TRUSTe Watchdog site.

Online Privacy Alliance (OPA)
http://www.privacyalliance.org

- The OPA plays a leading role serving as an industry coordinator to protect the rights of business relative to marketing, advertising, and maintenance of customer information files. The OPA is also a general information resource about privacy, and advocates a balance between consumers and businesses. Many of the industry members of the OPA provided resources and industry leadership in the creation of several of the self-regulatory seal programs seen on the Web today, including the TRUSTe program and the BBBOnLine Privacy Program. The TRUSTe program embodies principles that comply with fair information practices approved by the government and prominent industry-represented organizations. The BBBOnLine Privacy Program is similar to TRUSTe, but leans more toward protecting the interests of consumers versus business.

TRUSTe
http://www.truste.org

- In 1996, TRUSTe was founded as a non-profit organization dedicated to building global trust and confidence in the online environment. It soon emerged as a key initial response to the call for privacy self-regulation in the U.S. TRUSTe developed a program built upon the Fair Information Practices and the privacy guidelines established by the Online Privacy Alliance (OPA).

- TRUSTe is the most numerous privacy seal for providing assurance in the B2C marketplace. TRUSTe seals are priced from $600 to $13,000 annually (data as of February 2003).

- Under the terms of the general program, a licensee of the TRUSTe seal must, among other things, (1) complete a self-assessment and sign and attest to the statements made, (2) agree to display the TRUSTe Mark or Children's Mark on or linked to the privacy statement, (3) maintain and abide by a privacy statement that meets TRUSTe's approval, (4) disclose information use and collection practices, (5) abide by the minimum requirements of the program, (6) submit to compliance reviews, and (7) provide users a means to submit complaints.

- The TRUSTe Children's Seal Program extends privacy protection to children. Web sites whose online activities are directed at children under the age of 13 may apply for the special seal, abide by the Children's program requirements, and display TRUSTe's Children's Mark. TRUSTe states that the program meets the requirements of the Children's Online Privacy Protection Act (COPPA), which became effective in April 2000.

Privacy Advocacy Groups

Electronic Privacy Information Center (EPIC)

http://www.epic.org

- EPIC is a public interest research center in Washington, DC. It was established in 1994 to focus public attention on emerging civil liberties issues and to protect privacy, the First Amendment, and constitutional values. The EPIC Web site contains some interesting resources and links, including EPIC Privacy Litigation Docket, EPIC Policy Archives, and EPIC Online Guide to Congress' Privacy and Cyber-Liberties Bills.

Center for Democracy and Technology (CDT)

http://www.cdt.org

http://www.privacyexchange.org

- The CDT is a Washington, DC-based organization that promotes free speech and personal privacy in the digital arena. It is a nonprofit public interest organization that works for public policies that advance civil and democratic values in new computer and communications technologies. A valuable product of the CDT is the Privacy Exchange.

- The Privacy Exchange is an online global resource for privacy and data protection laws, practices, issues, trends, and developments worldwide. It (1) provides timely information on national data protection laws, regulations, standards, and practices, (2) collects and distributes model policies, agreements, and codes, and (3) encourages and expands international dialogue on consumer services and privacy protection. The Trans-Border section of the site contains both analyses of the laws impacting trans-border data flow and the actual experiences of companies transferring data under these laws. There are country-by-country summaries of legal requirements in the "Current National Law Requirements" section. Also included are model contracts and clauses for the protection of personal data in trans-border data flow.

APPENDIX C
LESSONS LEARNED
FROM PRIVACY DEBACLES

There have been numerous privacy debacles in recent years. The following list summarizes the lessons learned from common themes in those events and presents some ideas of actions to take, particularly for an organization that is just starting to address privacy issues or develop policy. It also includes recent examples that have been cited in the popular and technical press.

- Say What You Do and Do What You Say — Ensure that all privacy policy statements posted on a Web site are supported by actual practices. Conduct periodic reviews of policies and practices to ensure consistency across business units, and that practices comply with those policies. For larger organizations, this may mean developing an internal privacy compliance process. In the absence of privacy laws and regulations, the U.S. Federal Trade Commission has brought actions under deceptive trade practices laws. This is also applicable to liquidations of assets in bankruptcy or when organizations or their assets are bought and sold. In summer 2001, concerns were raised about the bankruptcy of Egghead.com and their consumer lists.

- Do the Right Thing — Serious consideration should be given to doing what is right or ethical in regard to privacy, as opposed to what is legally permissible. Numerous privacy issues have been tried in the court of public opinion where the penalty is loss of trust and possible activist reaction. Although perhaps not illegal, public reaction to knowledge that their activities were tracked when clicking on ads can be extremely negative.

- Patch Security Holes in Operating Systems — A number of issues arise because vendors of well-known computing platforms release their operating systems with inherent security weaknesses. Additionally, organizations fail to apply the patches to the security holes as quickly as hackers exploit them. Proactively monitor your operating system supplier by signing up with their automatic notification processes for any known security weaknesses and associated fixes. When the Code Red worm was active in August 2001, the operating system patches required had been widely available for some time and the industry press was full of warnings, yet hundreds of thousands of machines were not updated.

- Prevent Exposed E-mail Lists — When sending e-mail to a user list, privacy has been lost by inadvertently exposing the full mailing list to all addressees. Use standard agents to generate mailing lists and test to make sure that the software blind copies all recipients instead of printing out their full e-mail addresses.

- Examine URL Contents — Some Web sites redirect users to affiliated sites and include personally identifying information (PII) in the URL. Examine all links external to the Web site and use a packet sniffer to ensure the URL contents do not contain PII, especially if this is not disclosed in the privacy policy.

- Avoid PC/User ID Tags that Can Track Machines/Users — A number of organizations have raised the hackles of consumer privacy advocates by tagging software registration wizards or online transactions with a unique ID, including a GUID Processor Serial Number, or other identifying number that can be used to profile a user. Use a packet sniffer to ensure an ID tag is not being sent to a Web site.

- Avoid Web Bugs or at Least Disclose Their Use — While cookies can be managed by the browser or cookie management products, Web bugs, 1x1 pixel objects loaded from a third-party Web site, profile a user in such a way that they are unaware and cannot opt out. Examine the source of Web pages for 1x1 pixel objects loaded from a third-party Web site.

- Avoid Software that "Phones Home" — Software vendors sometimes engineer products to automatically send information back to the manufacturer. Test the registration procedures of all purchased software diligently, including what is captured in cookies and in URLs. Examine software offline to determine if agents are active that can sense an Internet connection or attempt to place the computer in online mode. Inventory all software on the Web site and ensure any data transferred off the Web site is disclosed.

- Provide Choice — Many privacy issues have resulted from failure to provide meaningful choice in putting the individual in control of their information. The general rule is not to use PII for any secondary purposes unless the individual has been provided a choice as to how that information will be managed on their behalf.

- Cleanse Demonstration Software — Development teams often take a cut of a live customer database to use as test data or demo data when demonstrating to potential customers that new applications reflect reality. It is standard practice in most organizations, whether it is an official procedure or not. At a minimum, however, data and software quality assurance testing must include a checkpoint to remove live data, even if only being used internally.

- Test Third-party Software for Glitches — Follow the manual and test thoroughly. Don't assume installations from shrink-wrap are preset with the right options. As an example, shopping cart software that was installed incorrectly revealed customer names, addresses, and account numbers, provided you knew certain keyword searches.

- Protect PII Even More Diligently When Change is Occurring — When making major changes on your Web site it is important to keep traditional security and firewalls, as well as content management processes, active until the final transition. A Web site exposed employee e-mail accounts and encrypted passwords during domain name migration.

- Confirm Employees Know the Privacy Policy — Training and awareness of good privacy practices and policy is critical to ensuring compliance. Programs should include new hires, FAQs and regular updates to prevent social engineering, and inadvertent disclosure of personal data. A customer service technician revealed customer account information to an outside party despite policy restrictions against disclosing such data.

- Appoint a Chief Privacy Officer — Even if not full-time, assign responsibility for privacy policy compliance to an executive of the organization highly placed enough to wield influence. Ensure the function is adequately funded and promoted as something supported by the highest levels of the organization.

APPENDIX D
GLOSSARY*

Due to the continually expanding body of technology knowledge, new terms emerge almost daily. If you come across a term in this report that you are not familiar with, please go to http:// webopedia.com/ for the definition.

Access – (1) A specific type of interaction between a subject and an object that results in the flow of information from one to the other. (2) The ability and means necessary to approach, store, or retrieve data, to communicate with, or to make use of any resource of a computer or communications system.

Access Control – The process of allowing only authorized users, programs, or other computer systems (e.g., networks) to access the resources of a computer system.

Access Control List (ACL) – A list of users or systems authorized for specific access to an object.

Access Control Software – Software to prevent unauthorized access to a computer system and sensitive resources, such as data and programs, and to monitor and report security violations.

Administrative Security – Management constraints, operational procedures, accountability procedures, and supplemental controls established to provide an acceptable level of protection for sensitive data or resources.

Application – An information system that includes manual and computerized procedures for source transaction origination, data processing and record keeping, and report preparation.

Application Program – Software designed for a specific business purpose (such as accounts receivable, billing, or inventory control).

Assurance – An objective judgment that an appropriate balance exists between the cost of potential loss or risk against the cost of actions that must be taken to control the risk.

Australian Privacy Charter – Its preamble states: "A free and democratic society requires respect for the autonomy of individuals, and limits on the power of both state and private organizations to intrude on that autonomy… Privacy is a key value which underpins human dignity and other key values such as freedom of association and freedom of speech… Privacy is a basic human right, and the reasonable expectation of every person."
See: http://www.anu.edu.au/people/Roger.Clarke/DV/PrivacyCharter.html

Authorization – Approval of a transaction or action by the appropriate level of management.

Automated Controls – Programmed procedures designed to prevent or detect and correct errors or irregularities that could have an adverse impact on the organization's business activities.

Availability – A control objective that information and processes are available when needed.

Capability Maturity Model (CMM) – Carnegie Mellon's Software Engineering Institute (SEI) model for achieving quality in developing systems; considers five levels of organizational maturity, ranging from 1, ad hoc, to 5, optimizing.

CCITT (Comité Consultatif International Telephonique et Telegrahique) – An organization that sets international communication standards, specifically the universal protocol for sending FAX documents across phone lines. (ITU – International Telecommunications Union – the parent organization for the CCITT)

Children's Online Privacy Protection Act (COPPA) – Effective April 21, 2000, in the U.S., applies to the online collection of personal information from children under 13. The law spells out what a Web site operator must include in a privacy policy, when and how to seek verifiable consent from a parent, and what responsibilities an operator has to protect children's privacy and safety online.

CIO – Chief Information Officer.

CISO – Chief Information Security Officer.

Classification – Determination that information requires a specific degree of protection against unauthorized access. Classification is performed according to a stated policy.

CobiT – Control Objectives for Information and Related Technology. Promulgated by the Information Systems Audit and Control Association (ISACA). See: http://www.isaca.org

CoE – Council of Europe. See: http://www.coe.int

Communications – Electronic transfer of information from one location to another. Data communications refers to digital transmission, and telecommunications refers to analog and digital transmission, including voice and video.

Compliance – A control objective that refers to compliance with applicable laws and regulations governing the organization.

Computer Security – Protection of computers, services, and functions from hazards, providing assurance critical functions are correct; includes information integrity.

Computer-Assisted Auditing Technique (CAAT) – A process, program, or series of tests that works through an application system to determine that programs are processing transactions as intended, data integrity is preserved, etc.

Confidentiality – A control objective that usually refers to information regarding intellectual property, trade secrets, competitive plans, or national security; information that is not made available or disclosed to unauthorized individuals, entities, or processes.

Contingency – A procedure or facility to be used in case of some serious consequences.

Contingency Planning – Preparing and testing plans to address disaster or disruption recovery.

Control Characteristics – Refers to the classification of controls into categories according to useful criteria.

Control Environment – The attitude and actions of the board and management regarding the significance of control within the organization. The control environment provides the discipline and structure for the achievement of the primary objectives of the system of internal control. The control environment includes the following elements: integrity and ethical values;

management's philosophy and operating style; organizational structure; assignment of authority and responsibility; human resource policies and practices; and competence of personnel.

Control Framework – A recognized system of control categories that covers all internal controls expected in an organization. Control frameworks include COSO, CoCo, Cadbury, and others (IIA).

Control Objectives – Statements of the desired result or purpose to be achieved by implementing control procedures.

Controller – A device that directs transmission of data over a network; may be controlled by a program executed in a processor to which it is connected or a program in the device.

Controls – A policy, manual, or computerized procedure designed to provide reasonable assurance regarding achievement of objectives in effectiveness and efficiency of operations, reliability of financial reporting, and compliance with applicable laws and regulations.

Cookies – Small files placed into a user's browser by a Web site to track, use, and retain information.

CPO – Chief Privacy Officer.

Data – Term used to denote any or all numbers, letters, symbols, etc. which can be accepted, processed, or produced by a computer; source or raw data becomes information in processing.

Data Administration – Management activities primarily concerned with data modeling and documentation of data.

Data Dictionary/Directory System – A repository of definitions of data contained in a database. Typically includes the name, type, usage, field size, source of data, and the application programs authorized to access the data. Collectively referred to as a data dictionary.

Data Encryption – The usually reversible transformation of data from plaintext to ciphertext by a cryptographic technique; encryption may be employed as the basis of other security services.

Data Security – Protection of data from accidental or unauthorized modification, destruction, or disclosure through policies, organizational structure, procedures, awareness training, software, and hardware to ensure that data is accurate, available, and accessed only by those authorized.

Database – A stored collection of related data needed by organizations and individuals to meet their information processing and retrieval requirements.

Decrypt – To convert encrypted text by use of the appropriate key and transformation technique into its equivalent plaintext (cleartext).

DES (Data Encryption Standard) – An algorithm used to protect non-classified information developed by an IBM team in 1974 and adopted as a standard in 1977.

Detection Controls – Controls that detect and report something that went wrong.

Device – Any electronic or electromechanical machine or component that performs a function for a computer. Device always refers to hardware; a device driver refers to software.

Digital Signature – A digital code attached to an electronic message to uniquely identify the sender and guarantee that the individual sending the message is who he or she claims to be. Digital signatures are a key component of authentication schemes for electronic commerce. To be effective, digital signatures must be unforgeable. A number of different encryption techniques are used to provide this level of security. See also *Encryption*.

Disclosure – A control objective specifying fair reporting and presentation of financial information.

Discretionary Controls – Those controls subject to human discretion.

Domain – A group of computers and devices on a network, administered as a unit with common rules and procedures. Internet domains are defined by the *IP address*, and devices sharing a common part of the IP address are said to be in the same domain.

Eavesdropping – Listening to phone calls or electronic messages without authorization from parties to the call or message.

E-commerce (Electronic Commerce) – Commercial activities conducted over the Internet.

EDI (Electronic Data Interchange) – The electronic exchange of business information between organizations using a standardized structured format.

Edit – An input control technique used to detect data that is inaccurate, incomplete, or unreasonable; performed either before or during regular processing.

Effectiveness – A control objective specifying that information should be relevant and pertinent to the business process, delivered in a timely, correct, consistent, and usable manner.

Efficiency – A control objective that concerns the provision of information through the most productive and economical use of resources.

Electronic Filters – Program function that can organize messages (typically e-mail) into categories and priorities.

Electronic Mail (E-mail) – The transmission of messages over electronic media.

Encoding – The digital representation of numbers, text, images, sound, or other information.

Encryption – The usually reversible transformation of data from plaintext to ciphertext by a cryptographic technique to increase confidentiality; may be the basis of other security services.

End-user Computing (EUC) – User-created, maintained, and operated systems that are outside of traditional information systems control.

Entity – Persons, objects, events, and locations that can be described by data elements or attributes.

Enterprise Risk Management – The processes used to identify, assess, and evaluate risks so mitigating controls can be put in place at appropriate cost in relation to their benefits.

EPIC (The Electronic Privacy Information Center) – See: http://www.epic.org/

EU (European Union) – See: http://europa.eu.int.

European Union Data Directive – Directive 95/46/EC of the European Parliament and of the Council of 24 October 1995 on the protection of individuals with regard to the processing of personal data and on the free movement of such data.
See: http://www.privacy.org/pi/intl_orgs/ec/eudp.html

Facsimile (FAX) – Communications in which documents are scanned, transmitted via a dialup phone line; device operations typically follow CCITT standards for information transmission – Group 1 analog, page transmission in 4 or 6 minutes; Group 2 analog, in 2 or 3 minutes; and Group 3 digital, with page transmission in less than one minute.

FCC (Federal Communications Commission) – The regulatory body for all U.S. interstate telecommunications services and international service that originates in the U.S, created under the U.S. Communications Act of 1934; the president appoints its board of commissioners.

FTC (Federal Trade Commission) – The regulatory body whose primary legislative mandate is to enforce the Federal Trade Commission Act, which prohibits unfair methods of competition and unfair or deceptive acts or practices in or affecting commerce.

File Transfer Protocol (FTP) – The Internet protocol for sending files.

Firewall – A combination of hardware and software that filters traffic to and from the Internet, and internally in some systems, for security purposes.

Functionality – A control objective specifying that a system should include all relevant capabilities, and be reasonably easy to use.

Gramm-Leach-Bliley (GLB) or Financial Services Modernization Act – In the U.S., GLB requires financial institutions (any enterprise engaged in financial activities, including insurance companies) to establish written policies for protection of customer information. Such policies are required to: assure the security and confidentiality of nonpublic personal information, protect against threats to its integrity or security, and protect against unauthorized access or use.

Hacker – Unauthorized person(s) outside the enterprise who intentionally, or maliciously, intend to break into the enterprise's information systems.

Health Insurance Portability and Accountability Act (HIPAA) – Provides requirements for storage and use of confidential or sensitive medical data in the U.S.; a national privacy bill to set policies for the legal use of identifiable health information, including access to personal medical information, an individual's rights regarding his or her information, and what constitutes inappropriate access.

Home Page – The Web page your browser is set to when you initiate an Internet session.

Imaging – Capturing, storing, and retrieving information regardless of its original format using the capabilities of optical disk technologies; digitizes and compresses a paper document, photograph, or other representation into a bit-map or raster image.

IMAP (Internet Message Access Protocol) – A method of accessing electronic mail or bulletin board messages that are kept on a mail server.

Information Security – As used in the *SAC* reports, information security refers to the characteristics of information and related systems and networks that ensure appropriate levels of confidentiality, integrity, and availability.

Infrastructure – The systems and resources necessary to support the operation of higher order systems, operations, organizations, industries, governments, economies, and the like.

Integrated System – A system in which either input or generated information updates the data files used by more than one application system.

Integrity – A control objective specifying complete, accurate, timely, and authorized processing.

Internal Audit Activity – The activity of a department, division, team of consultants, or other practitioner(s) that provides independent, objective assurance and consulting services designed to add value and improve an organization's operations. Internal auditing helps an organization accomplish its objectives by bringing a systematic, disciplined approach to evaluate and improve the effectiveness of risk management, control, and governance processes.

Internal Control – Procedures and tools an organization uses to assist in risk reduction; functions of internal controls protect or detect and remedy problems.

Internet – An international network composed of thousands of government, commercial, and academic networks. Formerly Arpanet.

Internet Protocol (IP) – Part of the TCP/IP protocols to track Internet address of nodes, route message, and recognize incoming messages; used in gateways to connect networks at OSI network Level 3 and above.

Internet Service Provider (ISP) – An institution that provides access to the Internet.

Internet Systems – Application functions for public use; entrusted to external providers.

Intrusion Detection Systems – A monitoring system to detect potential security violations by applying expertise based on pattern recognition, expert systems, and other technologies.

IP Address – An identifier for a computer or device on a TCP/IP network. Networks using TCP/IP route messages based on the IP address of the destination. The IP address format is a 32-bit numeric address written as four numbers separated by periods. (See *IP Number*) The numbers in an IP address are used to identify a particular network and a host on that network.

IP Number – A unique number with four parts separated by dots to identify every machine on the Internet; format: 123.321.456.1. (See also *IP Address*) Each number can be zero to 255. Within isolated networks IP addresses can be assigned at random, as long as each is unique. But connecting a private network to the Internet requires using registered IP addresses (or Internet addresses) to avoid duplicates. Domain name services translate domain names into IP addresses.

Kerberos – Security system developed at MIT to authenticate user's identity at logon, then used throughout the session. Based on private key encryption using the DES algorithm. Does not provide authorization to services or databases.

Key Card (also Smart Card) – An integrated circuit in a package approximately the size of a credit card that works with a challenge/response type of authentication system.

Key Management – Procedures dealing with the generation, storage, secure distribution, and application of encryption keys in accordance with security policy.

Layer – In the OSI reference model, network functions that comprise one level of a hierarchy.

Link Encryption – The use of data encryption on one or more links of a data communication system; implication is that data will be in cleartext in transfer or connection components.

Link Layer – The logical entity in the OSI model concerned with transmission of data between adjacent network nodes; second layer in the OSI model, between physical and network layers.

Log – A record of the events within a session; includes time and duration of the event, users accessing the system, and resources used in processing.

Logical – In information technology, a conceptual representation that may, or may not, coincide with the physical environment.

Logical Access Controls – Method for restricting access to programs and data using rules or algorithms, identification and authentication techniques. Contrast with physical access controls.

Logical Data Model – Refinement of the conceptual data model into well-defined representations of the data requirements and their attributes.

Logical Security – Software-based security and supporting policies and procedures to protect data from unauthorized destruction, manipulation, or disclosure. Does not address physical threats. See *Physical Security*.

Maintainability – A control objective to assure continuity and adaptability to change.

Mapping – In network operations, the logical association of one set of values, such as addresses on the network, with quantities or values of another set, such as devices on another network.

Masking of Passwords – Preventing passwords from appearing on screen or in output.

Message Authentication Code – A security technique that prevents unintentional or unauthorized alteration of information. Using an authentication algorithm, it is calculated based on the content of the message; transmitted with the message and verified on receipt.

Monitoring Controls – Identify undesirable events after they occur; check, supervise, or record progress of an activity, action, or system on a regular basis to identify change.

Network – Communications medium and components to transfer information; may include hosts, packet switches, telecommunications controllers, key distribution, access control centers, technical control devices, and others.

Network Architecture – Design principles, including organization of functions and description of data formats and procedures; the basis for the design and implementation of a network.

Network Firewall – A device that isolates or separates a network segment from the main network; filters network traffic between networks based on criteria.

Network Management – Monitoring of an active network to diagnose problems and gather statistics for network administration and fine-tuning.

Network Management Systems – Equipment and related software used in monitoring, controlling, and managing a data communications network.

Network Security – Protection of networks and their services from hazards; assurance that the network performs its critical functions correctly and there are no harmful side effects. Includes providing for information accuracy. See *Security*.

Network Security Domain – A contiguous region of a network that operates under a single, uniform security policy.

NIST (National Institute of Standards and Technology) – Assists U.S. industries in developing technology to improve product quality; custody of national measurement standards. See: http://www.nist.gov/

NSA (National Security Agency) – Operates U.S. Defense Department's Computer Security Center; collects national security intelligence; ensures communications and computer security within the U.S. government. See: http://www.nsa.gov/

OECD (Organization for Economic Cooperation and Development) – The OECD groups 30 member countries sharing a commitment to democratic government and the market economy. With active relationships with some 70 other countries, NGOs, and civil society, it has a global reach. Best known for its publications and statistics, its work covers economic and social issues from macroeconomics, to trade, education, development, and science and innovation. See: http://www.oecd.org/

Online Transaction Processing System (OLTPS) – See *Transaction Processing*.

OSI (Open Source Initiative) – A nonprofit organization dedicated to managing and promoting the open source definition for software that allows programmers to read, redistribute, and modify the software source code.

Outsourcing – Contracting in-house services to an external vendor for periods of time determined by agreement, typically five to 10 years. In the context of IT, can relate to all aspects, including data center operations, application system development or maintenance, telecommunications, and end-user support. Audit services my also be outsourced.

Overhead – In communications, all information, such as control, routing, and error-checking characters, in addition to user-transmitted data – status or operational instructions, network routing information, as well as retransmission or messages received in error.

P3P (Platform for Privacy Preferences Project) – Privacy Web site that provides a service for users to enter personal privacy preferences that can be accessed by Web sites they use, rather than having to specify it for each one.

Partnering – Providing customers, suppliers, and competitors with selected, online access to what were traditionally considered internal systems.

Password – Code word to control access to protected elements such as data files, networks, terminals, libraries, or applications; a private character string used to authenticate identity.

Penetration – Successful compromise of a protected system or network.

Penetration Testing – A method of security testing that attempts to circumvent access controls; where penetrators work under no constraints other than those applied to ordinary users.

Personally Identifiable Information (PII) – Privacy generally refers to information that can be associated with a specific individual, or that has identifying characteristics that might be combined with other information to do so. PII is the definitive term that should be used consistently when referring to an individual's personally identifiable information in the privacy context.

Personnel Security – Procedures to ensure that all personnel who have access to sensitive information have the required authorization as well as all appropriate clearances.

Physical Security – Measures to provide physical protection of a system's assets against malicious attacks and accidents; includes locks, guards, and similar administrative mechanisms.

PING – A utility, used primarily for troubleshooting Internet connections, to determine whether a specific IP address is accessible. It sends a packet to the specified address and waits for a reply. Freeware and shareware PING utilities are available.

POP (Post Office Protocol) – Allows a user to dynamically access a mail drop on a server to retrieve mail that the server is holding for the specific user.

Preventive Controls – Controls that protect or safeguard from something that could go wrong.

Privacy – The ability of an individual or organization to control collection, storage, sharing, and dissemination of their information. The right to adequately secure and define authorized users of information or systems requiring protection from disclosure of personal information.

Privacy.org – A Web site dedicated to news and information about privacy; a joint project of The Electronic Privacy Information Center and Privacy International. See: http://www.privacy.org/

Protective Controls – Protective controls help keep undesirable events from occurring.

Protocol – Formal set of rules governing format, timing, sequence, and error control of messages on a data network; may include managing a communications link and/or contention resolution.

Protocol Analyzer – A specialized computer and program that hooks into a LAN and analyzes traffic, records and displays traffic data; for diagnosing network problems.

Real Time – Online processing systems that accept and process data immediately, or an electronic operation that is performed in the same time frame as its real-world counterpart.

Reliability – A control objective for systems to provide adequate information for management to operate the entity and exercise its financial and compliance reporting responsibilities.

Risk Analysis – Assessment, management, and process of communicating risks to determine how often hazardous events might occur and their magnitude.

Risk Assessment – An analysis of system assets and vulnerabilities to determine exposures. There are two basic forms: Qualitative Risk Analysis of system assets and vulnerabilities to establish an expected loss from certain events based on estimated probabilities of the occurrence and the value of affected assets. Quantitative Risk Analysis of system assets, threats, and vulnerabilities derives a descriptive or scalar assessment of exposure.

Safe Harbor – U.S. Department of Commerce Safe Harbor: See: http://www.export.gov/safeharbor/

Search Engine – Software that creates indexes of databases or Internet sites based on the titles of files, key words, or the full text.

Security – Mechanisms and techniques that control access to premises, assets, system hardware, software, and data to prevent unauthorized modification, destruction, denial of service, or theft. Security is both physical and logical.

Security Administration – Providing for all facets of the security of the computer facility and its resources, including hardware and software.

Security Audit – An independent review of system records and activities to test for adequacy of system controls, ensure compliance with established policy and operational procedures, and recommend any indicated changes in controls, policy, or procedures.

Security Policy – The set of laws, rules, and practices that regulate how an organization manages, protects, and distributes sensitive or critical information.

Server – A system entity (combination of hardware and software) performing services on behalf of clients. Generally, these are services or functions required by multiple users, such as database management, printing, and security administration.

Service Bureau – A company or organization providing computer and related facilities for data processing for different users.

Simple Mail Transport Protocol (SMTP) – A protocol for sending e-mail messages between servers. Most e-mail systems that use the Internet use SMTP. With SMTP, messages can be retrieved with an e-mail client using either POP or IMAP. In addition, SMTP is generally used to send messages from a mail client to a mail server. This is why you need to specify both the POP or IMAP server and the SMTP server when you configure your e-mail application.

Simple Network Management Protocol (SNMP) – A protocol used to gather activity information on a TCP/IP network for monitoring and statistical purposes.

Smart Card – A credit card with a built-in microprocessor and memory used as an ID or transaction card. Can be inserted into a reader to transfer data to and from a computer, or provide algorithmic codes based on a personal identification number.

Software Engineering Institute (SEI) – The Software Engineering Institute is a federally funded research and development center sponsored by the U.S. Department of Defense. The SEI contract was competitively awarded to Carnegie Mellon University in December 1984. The SEI staff has extensive technical and managerial experience from government, industry, and academia. See: http://www.sei.cmu.edu/

Spam – Verb: To send e-mail messages as a broadcast message to a large number of people. Noun: Junk e-mail.

Spyware – Software that assists some outside party in observing the activities of an Internet user without permission or knowledge.

Statement of Auditing Standard No. 70 (SAS 70) – Requirements under generally accepted auditing standards that auditors adhere to in performing third-party reviews of outsourced activities.

Storage – Descriptive of a device or medium that can accept, hold, and deliver data on demand.

T1 – The lowest level of the four-level, time-division multiplexing hierarchy for the telephone system in North America. T1 provides 24 channels of 64 Kbps bandwidth, for a total bandwidth of 1.544 Mbps. A T1 circuit can transport voice, video, data, and fax.

T3 – A T3 circuit carries, in one multiplexed signal stream, the equivalent of 28 T1 circuits. It provides 44.736 Mbps of bandwidth.

TCP/IP (Transmission Control Protocol/Internet Protocol) – Communications protocols that allow dissimilar systems to communicate, usually over the Internet. The TCP protocol controls transfer of the data, and IP protocol provides routing; related are FTP - File Transfer Protocol, SMTP - Simple Mail Transfer Protocol, and Telnet terminal emulation capability.

Telecommunications – The communication of all forms of information.

Teleconferencing – A meeting among two or more people locally or geographically dispersed that may involve the use of audio and/or video hardware and software.

Teleprocessing – Transmitting data by telephone circuits or other transmission equipment. This equipment may be directly linked with a computer or can be independent.

Transaction Processing – Transactions received may be grouped into batches by the system for later processing; when *on-line real-time*, master files are updated immediately on acceptance of data.

Transaction Trail – A sequence of related evidence retained during processing and referenced after an event to reconstruct how information in reports, data files, or other records was created. Typically allows a person to evaluate propriety of original data input, subsequent processing/ summarization, application of programmed and manual modifications to data, etc.

Transmission Control Protocol (TCP) – Protocol used to place data into packets (and regroup incoming data), manage transmission of packets, and check for errors. TCP is the transport layer, a portion of the TCP/IP protocol that governs exchange of data.

TRUSTe – An independent, nonprofit privacy initiative dedicated to building users' trust and confidence on the Internet and accelerating growth of the Internet industry. TRUSTe developed a third-party oversight "seal" program to alleviate users' concerns about online privacy, while meeting the specific business needs of licensed Web sites. The TRUSTe program is backed by an assurance process to establish Web site credibility, and make users more comfortable when making online purchases or providing personal information. See: http://www.truste.org/

Trusted – Trusted nodes and systems are considered secured by other systems on the network. Untrusted nodes and systems are not secured and should require a user from that system to be identified and authenticated before access is granted.

Trusted Computer System – All protection within a computer system, including hardware, firmware, and software, responsible for enforcing security policy to create a protected environment and user services required. A trusted computing base (TCB) can enforce security policy only when mechanisms are designed effectively and parameters input correctly.

URL (Uniform Resource Locator) – The address of an Internet resource that is part of the World Wide Web.

User – Any person who interacts directly with a computer at the application level; programmers and other technical personnel are not considered users. Also refers to an individual who is accountable for an identifiable set of activities in a computer system.

User Datagram Protocol (UDP) – A connectionless protocol that, like TCP, runs on top of IP networks. Unlike TCP/IP, UDP/IP provides few error recovery services, offering instead a direct way to send and receive datagrams over an IP network. It is used primarily for broadcasting messages.

Utility Systems – Software that performs such tasks as copying, sorting, and merging files; system and data security control; peripheral device control (such as printers); and data storage.

Validation – The determination of the correctness, with respect to user needs and requirements, of the final data recorded in a system.

Virtual Private Network (VPN) – A service in which the public network can be used similar to private lines through use of encryption to protect data, with error testing and higher speed transmission. A VPN eliminates the need for fixed point-to-point private lines because it provides on-demand dialup bandwidths that can be dynamically allocated.

Virtual Storage – Using software and secondary storage devices to divide programs into smaller segments for transmission to and from internal storage, increasing its effective size.

Virus – A malicious, unauthorized, self-replicating computer program; parasitic in that it copies itself from and to another program and or system environment.

Web Bugs – One-pixel units capable of tracking users' activities on a Web page.

Web Page – A document created with HTML available on the World Wide Web.

WWW (World Wide Web) – Internet service that uses hypertext transport protocol (http) as the interface.

* Selected terms used with permission from The IIA's Professional Practices Framework, copyright 2002.

* Selected terms adapted from 1986 *Data Communications* Magazine. Copyright 1986 McGraw-Hill, Inc. All rights reserved.

* Selected terms adapted with permission of the Computer Security Institute from *Computer Security Journal,* copyright 1986.

IIA Research Foundation
Board of Research Advisors

The Institute of Internal Auditors Research Foundation

IIA RESEARCH FOUNDATION

Chairman's Circle

AT&T Corporation
Cargill, Inc.
Entergy Services, Inc.
ExxonMobil Corporation
JCPenney Company, Inc.
Microsoft Corporation
PricewaterhouseCoopers LLP
Southern Company Services, Inc.

The Institute of Internal Auditors Research Foundation